THE ESSENTIAL IT'S A WONDERFUL LIFE

The Essential

IT'S A WONDERFUL LIFE

A SCENE-BY-SCENE GUIDE TO THE CLASSIC FILM

MICHAEL WILLIAN

CHICAGO
REVIEW
PRESS

An A Cappella Book

Library of Congress Cataloging-in-Publication Data

Willian, Michael.

The essential It's a wonderful life : a scene-by-scene guide to the classic film / Michael Willian.

p. cm.

ISBN-13: 978-1-55652-636-7

ISBN-10: 1-55652-636-9

1. It's a wonderful life (Motion picture) I. Title.

PN1997.I758W55 2006

791.43'72--dc22   2006017588

Cover photo: *It's a Wonderful Life*, 1946. RKO/MPTV
Cover design: Sarah Olson
Line drawings: Brian Daniel
Photos on pages 51 and 120 are courtesy of the Academy of Motion Picture Arts and Sciences.

© 2004, 2006 by Michael Willian
All rights reserved
Originally published by Kerpluggo Books
Second edition published in 2006 by
Chicago Review Press, Incorporated
814 North Franklin Street
Chicago, Illinois 60610
ISBN-13: 978-1-55652-636-7
ISBN-10: 1-55652-636-9
Printed in the United States of America
5 4 3 2 1

For my parents

CONTENTS

INTRODUCTION

What is it about this film? There's no denying it's a classic. But over the past sixty years, *It's a Wonderful Life* has somehow managed to transcend mere artistic expression, weaving its way into the very fabric of our holiday ritual. For countless Americans, getting into the proper holiday spirit goes hand in hand with watching George Bailey's epic struggle to find love, contentment, and his purpose in life.

But what exactly makes this film so alluring? On the most basic level, sheer exposure has certainly played a role. This film led a rather unheralded existence until the mid-1970s, when the studio that owned the film forgot to file the requisite copyright renewal papers. This administrative oversight led television stations across the country to believe that they could show the film gratis. And show it they did, over and over again. It didn't take long before Pavlovian forces had us associating *It's a Wonderful Life* with our holiday experience.

Probing deeper, several of the film's themes speak to us on varying levels. The time-honored story of Good triumphing over Evil, using love, friendship, and old-fashioned values to defeat the Potters of the world. George and Mary's romantic journey, one that, in the end, has us yearning for the very things that George wants to throw away. The film's honest portrayal of the common man's pursuit of the sometimes elusive "American dream." Is that sympathy or empathy we feel for George as his life's dreams go unpursued?

But perhaps the film's greatest gift is its central message. *It's a Wonderful Life* serves as a much-needed annual reminder of the profound and positive impact that each of us has on the lives of others. At a time of year when perspective is at a premium, the film gently forces us to concede yet again that, hey, life really ain't all that bad after all!

Whatever the allure, one thing is certain: with each December viewing, the film seems as familiar to you as an old friend. And why shouldn't it? After all, you've seen it enough times. You know most of the lines. And you surely know an amusing anecdote or two about the film or have a favorite scene detail that you keep an eye out for each year.

But how well do you *really* know it? Well, trust us—there is much, much more to learn about this film. With this guide, our goal is to breathe new life into this friend, clueing you in to the veritable treasure trove of anecdotes and items of intrigue that have managed to elude you all these years. We do this by walking you through the film, scene by scene, in a fun, insightful, and occasionally offbeat manner. We provide in-depth discussions of film details, curiosities, gaffes, anecdotes, historical tie-ins, strange lines, and countless other things you've never noticed before. In the end, we assure you, you will come away with a newfound appreciation for the film and its actors.

So if you think you know this film, think again. We invite you to kick back, pop in your VHS or DVD, grab the remote, and join us as we put this film under the microscope for you.

USING THIS GUIDE

Before we dive headlong into the fun stuff, here are a few words on how to use the guidebook. To warm up, we recommend first checking out the film chronology that we developed for you. It clarifies the sequence and timing of events in the film, which we find can be a little confusing. With this overview fresh in your mind, you'll be ready for a full frontal attack on the film.

We have organized the film into chapters based on the relation of scenes either temporally or from a plot standpoint. Each chapter begins with an overview of the scenes discussed. Each scene overview is followed by topics relating to events that occur in the chapter. We organized topics into the following headings: Closer Looks, Did You Know?, History Lesson, Just Wondering, Film Anecdotes, Cast Anecdotes, Music Notes, Random Thoughts, and Explanation Required. Topics are discussed sequentially as much as possible so you won't have to jump around too much within a chapter.

The guidebook makes for a great read all by itself. We provide plenty of context for the items discussed, so you don't need to actually watch the film to figure out what we're talking about. Of course, you won't be able to see for yourself some of the visual oddities that we point out, but you'll be clued in to them the next time you watch the film.

If you're looking for instant gratification, you'll definitely want to have the film handy as you read the guidebook. Since there are so many things to check out, we recommend taking a chapter-by-chapter approach. Before each chapter, read all of the corresponding topics. Then watch the scenes for that chapter, looking for the visual stuff that we've pointed out. Most of the stuff you'll catch on the first run through, but there will be plenty of things that you'll want to examine more closely using freeze frame or slow motion. (Keep in mind that the screen resolution of some televisions may make it tougher to see some of the more detailed things we point out.) And don't forget to use the DVD bookmarks that we have provided, as they will give you instant access to your favorite scenes and items of interest.

Our favorite guidebook features are the maps and diagrams of downtown Bedford Falls, downtown Pottersville, the Building & Loan offices, and George and Mary's house. Trying to orient yourself in these settings through casual viewings is no easy thing, particularly for the downtown scenes. So we have done the heavy lifting for you, painstakingly analyzing and reconstructing the set designs so that you can see for the first time the location of key set features such as streets, stores, offices, rooms, and even furniture.

Even better, each map and diagram has its own numbered index that enables you to see where your favorite scenes take place relative to each other. How cool is that? These maps and diagrams offer a whole new level of insight into the film, and we encourage you to refer to them early and often.

The guidebook also shines some light on the film's largely overlooked musical score, a hodgepodge of original score material and popular songs that, in the end, works quite well. Not only do we discuss intriguing aspects of the score under the Music Notes topic heading, we also provide a breakdown of the score, including the names of songs and where they appear in the film.

Finally, we've included an *It's a Wonderful Life* quiz, designed to separate the contenders from the pretenders and settle once and for all how well you and your friends really do know this film. But if you really want a true test, you're going to have to take the quiz *before* you read the guidebook, since the answers to some quiz questions are necessarily disclosed in our topic discussions. We found that the best way to use the quiz is with a group, either while watching the film or just lounging around the house enjoying the holidays. Just take turns acting as quizmaster, and let the head scratching begin!

FILM CHRONOLOGY

Following the film's story line can be tricky given that it spans three decades, contains numerous jumps in time, and discloses a fair amount of background information through throwaway dialogue. Adding to the confusion is the fact that the film's director, Frank Capra, opted against using makeup to visibly age Jimmy Stewart and Donna Reed. Thus, George and Mary look just as fresh faced in December 1945 as they do at the graduation dance in 1928. Finally, while many scenes contain clues to the year and month they are set in, the timing of some scenes can be pegged only by referencing the film's production materials.

So to help give you a better perspective of how the story unfolds, we have put together a handy scene chronology. Nothing fancy here. Just a quick overview to get you oriented.

CHRISTMAS EVE 1945: The film picks up in Bedford Falls at 9:45 P.M., one hour before George arrives on the bridge contemplating suicide. The opening scenes cover the prayers of George's friends and family and the angels in heaven assigning Clarence the task of saving George.

WINTER 1919: The retrospective of George's life starts with a look back at the winter day in 1919 when George rescues Harry after he falls through the ice during a sledding excursion. George is twelve at the time of the accident; Harry is nine.

MAY 1919: Later that spring, George saves Mr. Gower from certain ruin by intercepting a prescription that Mr. Gower has accidentally filled with poison capsules.

JUNE 1928: Nine years later, George is preparing to leave the next day on a much-anticipated trip overseas. George, now twenty-one or twenty-two, deferred going to college and has spent the last few years helping his dad run the Building & Loan. Mary, now eighteen, is graduating from high school. This single day covers: George at the luggage shop, George visiting Mr. Gower at Gower Drugs, George walking through downtown Bedford Falls, George at home with his family, Harry's graduation dance, and George walking Mary home after the dance.

SEPTEMBER 1928: Three months later, George is scheduled to catch a train for college immediately after he attends a meeting of the Building & Loan's board of directors, at which a successor to George's father will be appointed.

JUNE 1932: Four years later, Harry returns from college. George, now twenty-five or twenty-six, has been waiting for Harry to come home and take over for him at the Building & Loan. Mary, now twenty-two, is just back from college. This single day covers: George and Uncle Billy meeting Harry at the train station, Harry's "welcome home" party at Mrs. Bailey's house, George encountering Violet downtown, and George calling on Mary.

OCTOBER 1932: Four months later, George and Mary get married. Their wedding day covers: the wedding send-off, the bank run scenes, and George and Mary in the "bridal suite."

JUNE 1934: Twenty months later, George and Mary help the Martinis move from Potter's Field to Bailey Park. This single day covers: the Martini's move, Potter meeting with his rent collector, George meeting with Potter to discuss possible employment, and George returning home later that night to learn that Mary is pregnant.

JUNE 1934–SEPTEMBER 1945: The next eleven years are covered by montages—first a "Bailey family" montage and then a "war years" montage. George and Mary's first two children are born before World War II starts (meaning before September 1939). The youngest two Baileys arrive during the war, which officially ends in September 1945.

CHRISTMAS EVE 1945 (REPRISE): Still in flashback mode, we return to the day that George contemplates suicide. George is around forty; Mary around thirty-six. The daytime scenes cover: George spreading word of Harry's return from the war, Uncle Billy losing the bank deposit, Violet stopping by the Building & Loan for a favor from George, and George and Uncle Billy searching for the bank deposit.

George arrives home on Christmas Eve around 6:00 P.M. and storms out of the house fifteen minutes later. Between 6:15 P.M. and 10:45 P.M., George makes stops at Potter's office and Martini's. At precisely 10:45 P.M., George arrives on the bridge.

We are now officially back to the present. From 10:45 P.M. to around 11:45 P.M., George "rescues" Clarence and takes a whirlwind tour of Pottersville. George then returns to Bedford Falls, runs home from the bridge, and reunites with his family at five minutes to midnight.

THE ESSENTIAL IT'S A WONDERFUL LIFE

1

THE ANGELS CONSPIRE TO SAVE GEORGE

66 Please, God. Something's the matter with Daddy. **99**
—JANIE BAILEY

W e begin our journey by eavesdropping on the urgent prayers of
several Bedford Fallsians this Christmas Eve 1945. In order, we hear
from Mr. Gower, Mr. Martini, Mrs. Peter Bailey, Bert the cop, Ernie the taxi
driver, Mary Bailey, Janie Bailey, and Zuzu Bailey. The common theme of
these prayers? George Bailey is in trouble and could use some help from
above, and fast. For reasons that will be made known to us shortly, George
has convinced himself that "he's worth more dead than alive." And on his
current course, he'll be putting this theory to the test just as soon as he can
find a bridge suitable for jumping.

Enter the angels, who have heard this chorus of prayers and are now
scrambling to come up with an intervention plan. The head angel and his
assistant, Joseph, eventually assign good old Clarence to the project. Joseph
doesn't have much confidence in Clarence's abilities, but we know better—
Clarence is just the right man for the job. All Clarence needs is a little background on this Bailey character, and he and Joseph begin by reviewing a few
defining moments from George's youth.

In the first of two such vignettes, we find George and his pals sledding
down a riverbank during the winter of 1919. Everything is going swell until
George's younger brother, Harry, eager to prove himself equal to the task,
pushes off a little too hard, overshoots the bailout zone, and tumbles through
an opening in the ice. George instantly jumps in after his brother and implores
the other boys to help pull them out. Thanks to George's quick thinking, Harry
will be around at the end of the film to toast his older brother!

1

The second vignette from George's youth is the infamous "poison capsules" incident at Gower Drugs. It is now late spring 1919, and George has recovered from last winter's sledding mishap, though he does have permanent hearing loss in one ear. George is working as Mr. Gower's store hand, and by all accounts he is an honest, hardworking young boy, if also a bit of a dreamer.

After getting scolded by old man Gower upon his arrival, George waits on two young girls, Violet Bick and Mary Hatch, both of whom will be vying for George's attention for years to come. There are some hints as to which girl will eventually win out, but it's going to be a while before George figures it out for himself.

While tending to Mary's order, George stumbles across a telegram containing news that Mr. Gower's son has died suddenly and under tragic circumstances. George suspects that all is not well with Mr. Gower in the back room and decides to investigate. Sure enough, Mr. Gower is stone drunk, and worse yet, he's filling prescriptions with poison capsules! This is not good. George is not sure how to handle this rather delicate situation, so he hightails it over to his dad's office at the Bailey Brothers Building & Loan Association.

Unfortunately, there's trouble brewing at the Building & Loan too. Henry F. Potter, the "meanest and richest man in town" and the Building & Loan's chief competition in the Bedford Falls real estate market, is in the house for a business meeting, and, invariably, these meetings are contentious. George slips into the meeting to find his father arguing with Potter about a loan that Potter is holding over the Building & Loan's head. The exchange gets more and more heated, and when Potter calls George's father a "miserable failure," George steps in with a few choice words—and a gratuitous shove—for the wheelchair-bound Potter. George is quickly shown the door by his father; and so ends the first of many skirmishes to come between George and Potter.

Forced to solve the drugstore dilemma on his own, George returns to the store, where he takes some serious heat from Mr. Gower for failing to deliver the prescription. But eventually he confronts Mr. Gower with the facts—"you put poison in those capsules, you rummy!"

George's Friends and Family Pray For Him *(0:01:17)*

CLOSER LOOK: We're not even ten seconds into the film and we already have a gem for you. Take a close look at the shot accompanying Mr. Gower's prayer. It shows the downtown Bedford Falls street that George runs down on his way home at the end of the film. After a few seconds, a man appears in the boulevard's median running wildly and waving his right hand. *(0:01:29)*

That, folks, is most definitely George Bailey. So what gives here? Did director Frank Capra purposefully and sublimely synchronize the prayers with George's triumphant return home? Are George's friends and family supposed to be praying for him at the very moment he is headed home to see them?

We think not. Remember, in the next scene the angels hear and *respond* to the various prayers. And the angels' meeting in heaven occurs at 9:45 P.M. earth time (the head angel says George will be on the bridge at 10:45 P.M., prompting Clarence to remark that he only has "an hour to dress"). But George doesn't arrive home until 11:55 P.M., which would place him downtown around 11:45 P.M.

This leads us to conclude that George's cameo during the opening prayer scene is completely inadvertent. Our theory is that Capra needed a wintertime shot of the street in front of Gower Drugs to go with Mr. Gower's prayer and used an outtake from George's run through downtown, unaware that the seemingly actionless footage actually included Jimmy Stewart in midtake.

CLOSER LOOK: Accompanying the prayer of George's mother is a shot of a local church. *(0:01:37)* Look for this church later in the film across the street from where George crashes his car after leaving Martini's. *(1:37:34)* It's also visible when George returns to the scene of the accident in Pottersville. *(1:45:54)*

CLOSER LOOK: Bert's prayer is accompanied by a shot of a house, which presumably is supposed to be his. Later on in the guide we'll clue you in to the exact location of this house in Bedford Falls. For now, take a look at the very end of this clip, where you will see a mysterious man suddenly, and for no apparent reason, sprint off the front porch of the house next door. *(0:01:43)*

The Angels Talk in Heaven *(0:02:10)*

FILM ANECDOTES: Although the "head angel" is never actually mentioned by name in the film, the final script identifies this character as Franklin. This less-than-angelic-sounding name is a remnant of an earlier script that had Benjamin Franklin serving as the head angel and showed him talking to Joseph in heaven as he tinkered at a workbench with his latest invention. Thankfully, this cornball opening got the ax. This scene is just one of several that underwent major revisions for the better—we'll point a few more out along the way.

DID YOU KNOW? The creative seed for *It's a Wonderful Life* was a short story called *The Greatest Gift*. The author, Philip Van Doren Stern, originally

included the story in his Christmas card mailings and later sold it to RKO Radio Pictures for $10,000. The story needed a lot of work, though. It *began* with "George Pratt" contemplating suicide on the bridge and had him masquerading as a door-to-door brush salesman in Pottersville as he investigated life in his absence.

While the RKO rewrites contributed several key scenes—George saving Harry, George at Gower Drugs, George courting Mary on the night of the dance—they failed to capture the spirit of the original story. One script featured dueling Georges, with "good George" battling "bad George" to the death on the bridge. Another had Uncle Billy offing himself with a gun. Still, director Frank Capra was so convinced of the story's potential that he fronted his own money to buy it from RKO. He then hired several writers to whip the story into shape, before finishing off the job with his own Capraesque contributions. With so many contributors, credit for the screenplay ultimately had to be resolved through a Screen Writers Guild arbitration, with Capra and three of his writers prevailing to the exclusion of the RKO writers.

FILM ANECDOTES: Although *It's a Wonderful Life* received largely favorable reviews upon its release in December 1946, the film did not exactly take the box office by storm. According to *Variety* magazine, *It's a Wonderful Life* failed to crack the top 25 grossing films for 1947, coming in on the list tied for 26th at $3.3 million, compared to $11.5 million for the top grosser, *The Best Years of Our Lives*.

The film's performance at the 1946 Academy Awards was also a bit of a letdown. While the film did receive five Academy Award nominations, including Best Director, Best Picture, and Best Actor (Stewart), it came away empty-handed, losing four of the five awards to that year's film juggernaut, *The Best Years of Our Lives*.

It's a Wonderful Life was originally scheduled for release in January 1947, but at the last minute RKO moved up the release date to December 1946, thus making it eligible for the 1946 Academy Awards. Many believe that this maneuver worked against the film as the competition in 1947 was not quite as stiff. Whatever the case, a 1947 release date would have resulted in *It's a Wonderful Life* going toe to toe for Best Picture with its arch rival in the holiday film genre, *Miracle on 34th Street*.

George, Harry, and the Boys Go Sledding (0:04:01)

CLOSER LOOK: As the boys prepare to sled down the river bank, check out the patch on each boy's toboggan cap. It's a rather ominous skull and crossbones, which signifies a club that the boys all belong to. *(0:04:04)*

One of these boys is actually supposed to be Ernie—his turn sledding down the hill either was written out of the script just prior to filming or got cut in postproduction. Among the boys who are shown sledding is Sam, who gives his patented hee haw sign—the first of many more to come—before shoving off.

CLOSER LOOK: The boys are actually trespassing as they sled, and the land they are trespassing on belongs to the man that Bedford Fallsians love to hate, Henry F. Potter. Look for the sign that reads "No Trespassing—Henry F. Potter" right behind George as Harry sleds down the hill. *(0:04:43)*

FILM ANECDOTES: An early version of this scene had Harry facing the same peril, but under different circumstances. In that version, the boys play ice hockey on the river as Potter watches with disdain from his house. An errant shot by George breaks Potter's "No Trespassing" sign, and the puck settles on his property. Seeing this, Potter becomes enraged. Moments later, the gardener releases Potter's attack dogs on the boys, and in the ensuing chase Harry falls through the ice.

DID YOU KNOW? George's technique for rescuing Harry is a bit unorthodox, although you sure can't argue with the results. George shouldn't have jumped in after Harry. The cold water is dangerously debilitating, and George now faces the same problems getting out that Harry does.

Instead, George should first have tried to pull him out with one of the nearby shovels. That said, George's call for his pals to form a human chain (he yells, "Chain, gang!") was actually a good idea. Lying down and sliding out to the breakthrough area distributes body weight over a larger surface, thereby decreasing the likelihood that the rescuers will end up in the drink as well.

By the way, if you ever find yourself alone and in Harry's predicament, all is not lost, but a game plan is critical. Resources on ice safety seem to agree on the basic approach to a self-rescue. First and foremost, after you go in, remember to *breathe*. If you don't regain a somewhat normal breathing pattern after the shock of hitting the cold water, your chances of making it out are slim indeed. Next, locate the edge with the strongest ice, which, conveniently enough, is usually in the direction you approached from.

Then, collect any objects on you that can be used to claw into the ice (picture a polar bear clawing its way out of the water). Keys, a pen, a barrette, even a credit card, would come in handy here; otherwise, here's hoping you haven't cut your nails recently.

Now, get those arms fully extended onto the ice (you may have to punch away some weak ice to get to a solid edge), dig in with whatever you've got, let your body get horizontal in the water, start a swimmer's kick, and pull yourself up. Once you're out, to avoid an encore performance, don't forget to *roll away* from the hole.

George Waits on Mary and Violet at Gower Drugs *(0:05:08)*

FILM ANECDOTES: The beginning of this scene gives us our first glimpse of one of the film's most important characters, downtown Bedford Falls. The downtown set consisted of three and a half full-scale city blocks, complete with a boulevard lined with trees (supposedly transplanted just for the shoot). Different versions of the set were created to depict not only the aging of Bedford Falls (scenes in the town were set in 1919, 1928, 1932, and 1945), but also Bedford Falls' alter ego, Pottersville. The map of Bedford Falls, which we have painstakingly reconstructed from film footage and other sources, will clue you in to the spot where various scenes take place, as well as the location of various Bedford Falls business establishments.

CLOSER LOOK: Before showing up for work at Gower Drugs, George has been playing baseball with his pals. As the boys march through downtown, look for their mismatched uniforms and the assortment of baseball equipment that they're carrying, including several mitts, a bat, and a catcher's mask. *(0:05:10)*

CLOSER LOOK: Check out the writing on the mirror behind the soda fountain counter. It's an advertisement for the "Gower Special," which sells for twenty cents. *(0:06:12)* No word on what this "Special" is, but given Mr. Gower's shaky mental state, we're recommending that customers ask Mr. Gower to take the first bite!

CLOSER LOOK: It appears that young Violet has frequented Gower Drugs so often that George knows exactly what she's going to order—two cents' worth of shoelaces. Look for George actually ringing up two cents on the cash register. *(0:06:27)* We were hoping to catch a film gaffe here, with George ringing up a different amount, but no such luck.

HISTORY LESSON: In this scene we learn that by the age of twelve George had already developed a fascination with travel and world geography. The subject of coconuts sets George off on a diatribe about the South Seas. His fascination with this area of the world was fairly typical for the era. Americans were introduced to the culture of the South Seas and Pacific Islands in the early part of the twentieth century, primarily through fairs and expositions such as the Panama-Pacific International Exposition in San Francisco in 1915. Beginning in the late teens, Americans were clamoring for anything related to Hawaiian culture, and were particularly obsessed with Hawaiian music and the exotic and dreamy sounds of the ukulele and the Hawaiian (steel) guitar.

CLOSER LOOK: The following products and advertisements appear in Mr. Gower's drugstore during the "poison capsules" scenes—see if you can spot them:

- Coca-Cola
- Paterson tobacco pipes
- La Unica cigars
- Camel cigarettes
- Lucky Strike cigarettes
- Chesterfield cigarettes
- Vaseline hair tonic
- Penetro cough syrup
- Pepto-Bismol
- Bayer aspirin ("for colds and influenza")
- the *Saturday Evening Post*

EXPLANATION REQUIRED: Are you impressed by George's pronouncement that he's been "nominated for membership" in the National Geographic Society? What he really means is that he will soon have a subscription to the *National Geographic* magazine. Then, as now, by filling out a form included in the magazine and paying a few dollars, anyone could join the National Geographic Society.

The form simply called for a current member of the Society to "nominate" the prospective member for acceptance (the 1919 version of the form read, "Recommendation for Membership in the National Geographic Society"). Included in the membership was a subscription to the *National*

DOWNTOWN BEDFORD FALLS

1. Young George and his pals see Potter in his horse-drawn carriage (the carriage passes in front of the Building & Loan headed toward the court house).

2. The steps leading up to the Building & Loan.

3. George waves to Uncle Billy, Tilly, and Eustace, who are all yelling to him from a Building & Loan window.

4. George, Bert, and Ernie run into Violet after George picks up his suitcase (Violet crosses Jefferson Avenue walking toward the courthouse).

5. Violet spots George as she closes her beauty shop on the night of Harry's welcome home party.

6. George and Violet discuss making a night of it (shot looking away from the courthouse).

7. George, Mary, and Ernie observe a crowd gathering in front of the Bedford Falls Trust and Savings Bank on the day of the bank run.

8. Mr. Gower sells war bonds in front of the courthouse.

9. George hands Ernie and Mr. Gower newspapers on Christmas Eve announcing Harry's receipt of the Medal of Honor.

10. Uncle Billy salutes a military jeep on his way to the bank (shot looking toward the courthouse).

11. George and Uncle Billy retrace Uncle Billy's steps leading up to his visit to the bank (shot looking away from the courthouse).

12. George stands in front of "You Are Now in Bedford Falls" sign on his way home on Christmas Eve (shot looking toward the courthouse).

13. George wishes Potter a "Merry Christmas" on Christmas Eve as Potter sits in his office.

9

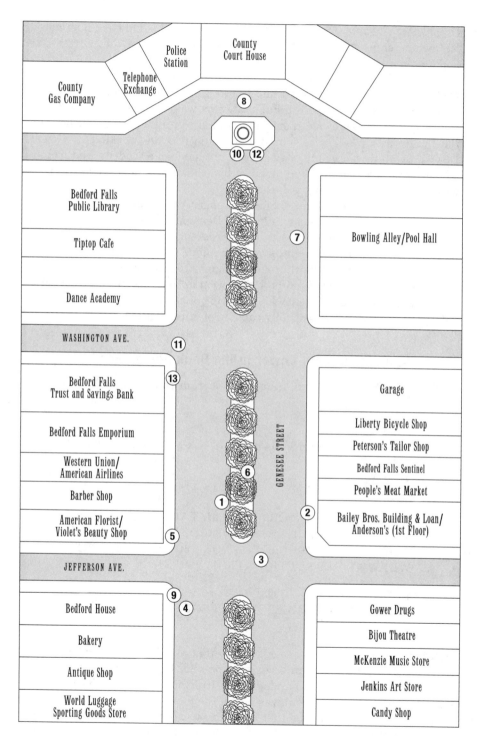

Geographic magazine. So while George's claim that he had been nominated for membership was no doubt accurate, in all likelihood the person who nominated him was his mother.

CAST ANECDOTES: Jimmy Stewart and Donna Reed both grew up in their own small-town versions of Bedford Falls. Stewart was born on May 20, 1908, in Indiana, Pennsylvania. He spent much of his youth helping his father run the family hardware store, not unlike young George working at Gower Drugs. By his own account, Stewart was not much of a student, and had an adventurous streak that found him as a little boy planning an African safari with the help of his indulgent father.

Reed was born Donna Belle Mullenger on January 27, 1921, just outside the small farming community of Denison, Iowa. The oldest of five, "Donnabelle" helped her parents keep order on the family farm. A true midwestern farm girl, Donna was a 4-H member, and at thirteen won a blue ribbon at the Iowa State Fair for a tasty batch of rolls. And lest there be any doubt about her farmhand skills, Donna won an impromptu bet with actor Lionel Barrymore (Mr. Potter) while shooting on location for *It's a Wonderful Life* when she proved herself fully capable of milking a cow.

Trouble with Mr. Gower in the Back Room *(0:07:29)*

CLOSER LOOK: Here's the text from the telegram that George finds by the register:

BEDFORD FALLS NY QAB 605 31 3EX MAY 3 1919 1211AM

MR EMIL GOWER
BEDFORD FALLS NY

WE REGRET TO INFORM YOU THAT YOUR SON ROBERT DIED VERY SUDDENLY THIS MORNING OF INFLUENZA STOP EVERYTHING POSSIBLE WAS DONE FOR HIS COMFORT STOP WE AWAIT INSTRUCTIONS FROM YOU STOP

EDWARD MELLINGTON
PRESIDENT HAMMERTON COLLEGE

HISTORY LESSON: While it may seem strange that Mr. Gower's college-aged son could die of the flu, such an occurrence was all too familiar to Americans back then. The Influenza Pandemic of 1918 (a pandemic is basically an epidemic of global proportion) was one of the most devastating plagues the world has ever seen. Dubbed the "Spanish flu" after a massive outbreak in Spain, one of the virus's earliest appearances in America came in spring

1918 at a military training camp in Kansas. By fall, the virus was in full swing, with nearly 200,000 Americans dying in October alone. All told, the virus afflicted one in four Americans and accounted for some 500,000 deaths. Worldwide the figures were staggering—one in five persons afflicted and an estimated 20 to 40 million deaths.

While most strains of influenza are fairly mild and pose a death threat only to the elderly and very young, this particular strain inexplicably proved most deadly for those between twenty and forty. Moreover, the strain struck with a quickness and severity not seen before or since. It was not uncommon for victims to develop fatal respiratory problems in a matter of hours.

Thus, Mr. Gower's son was a prime candidate for contracting this virus, and his sudden demise was entirely plausible. Still, from a historical perspective, the timing of his sickness is just a little off. Mr. Gower's son is stricken in May 1919, yet the deadly virus strain had all but disappeared by then. This story detail undoubtedly came from director Frank Capra as he himself was stricken by the virus while serving in the military in fall 1918.

CLOSER LOOK: Believe it or not, there are legitimate medicinal uses for poisons, so we will forgive Mr. Gower for having poison on hand. However, the specific type of poison that Mr. Gower filled the prescription with remains a mystery. On the back of the poison bottle several letters— LYCYR—are legible from a partially torn label. *(0:08:19)* These letters almost certainly refer to the plant *Glycyrrhiza glabra*, which is better known as licorice.

Well, you don't need a degree in pharmacology to know that licorice is not a poison. Back then druggists used licorice root to flavor medicines as well as to treat a variety of common ailments. All of this means that the prop guy probably just grabbed an old medicine bottle, slapped a poison label on one side and tried, with limited success, to peel off the licorice label on the other side.

CLOSER LOOK: As for the rest of the bottles in the back room, trying to read their labels is a frustrating exercise. Most of them are just a hair out of focus, and it doesn't help that these old apothecary bottles use arcane Latin abbreviations. Anyway, here's a list of the bottles that we can read, along with a brief description of their primary medicinal uses—see if you can spot them. If you can read any other labels, your eyes are better than ours!

PV CINCH AUB—references *Cinchona*, a genus of trees and shrubs native to South America. Bark is harvested for quinine, which is used to treat malaria.

SULPHUR—a natural element with antibacterial and antifungal qualities. Medicinal uses include treating forms of influenza, ear and throat infections, and various skin disorders.

CAMPHORA—Latin for camphor, a compound derived from the wood of a camphor tree. Medicinal uses include inducing perspiration and coughing.

R. ZINGIB.—references *Zingiber*, the botanical name for ginger. Medicinal uses include preventing nausea and motion sickness, and treating upset stomachs and indigestion.

CALAMINE—a powder derived from zinc oxide. Used medicinally in skin lotions to alleviate skin irritations caused by insect bites, poison ivy, sunburn, etc.

MYRISTICA—the botanical name for nutmeg. Has a calming effect on the nervous system. Used externally to treat sore muscles, rheumatism, and arthritis; internally for digestive disorders. Also used as a flavoring agent.

HISTORY LESSON: George reveals that Mr. Gower is *supposed* to be filling a prescription for treating diphtheria. Mr. Gower undoubtedly spent a great deal of time treating this insidious disease, which was a leading cause of death for children during this era. While some strides were made treating and preventing diphtheria during the first two decades of the twentieth century, a surefire vaccine was not developed until the mid-1920s.

Take our word for it—this disease is not something you want to contract. Diphtheria typically takes hold in the nose and throat. Early symptoms are innocuous enough—fever, chills, sore throat, enlarged lymph nodes—but within a few days, a coating of gray matter begins to build in the upper respiratory tract. If left unchecked the buildup will result in death by asphyxiation. Also, the toxin produced by diphtheria can cause paralysis and death by heart failure. If none of this sounds like fun, just remember to get that Td booster shot every ten years.

CLOSER LOOK: Keep an eye out for a minor film gaffe in this scene as Mr. Gower's cigar suddenly disappears from his mouth. *(0:08:33)* This gaffe, as with a few others in the film, is most likely attributable to some rough last-minute film editing.

CAST ANECDOTES: This is our first good look at old man Gower, Bedford Falls' town druggist—and town drunk! The down and out Mr. Gower is played by H. B. Warner, who was a regular in films directed by Frank Capra, having appeared in no less than four of them prior to *It's a Wonderful Life*: *Mr. Deeds Goes to Town* (1936), *Lost Horizon* (1937, nominated for Best Supporting Actor), *You Can't Take It with You* (1938), and *Mr. Smith Goes to Washington* (1939). Warner should have felt very much at home in the backroom of Gower Drugs given that he studied medicine before becoming an actor.

Early in his career, Warner had the distinction of playing Christ in Cecil B. DeMille's silent film classic, *The King of Kings* (1927). Film lore has it that DeMille was so obsessed with protecting the sanctity of the film that he forced Warner to agree to various "morality" provisions regulating his lifestyle and restricting the types of film roles he could take on. To DeMille's delight, no doubt, Warner's portrayal of the Savior King sent him down a career path cobbled with rather more serious characters. Some twenty years later, though, Capra gave Warner the chance to show his true grit; and Warner delivered, playing not just one, but two rummies (one in Bedford Falls and one in Pottersville) to inebriated, stubble-faced perfection.

George Seeks His Dad's Advice *(0:08:45)*

DID YOU KNOW? As George is wondering what to do about Mr. Gower and the poison capsules, he notices an advertisement in the drugstore that reads "Ask Dad, he knows," which prompts him to seek out his dad. This advertising slogan is for Sweet Caporal cigarettes and shows a fatherly figure puffing away on a smoke. It's unclear what "Dad" is supposed to "know," but whatever it is, it's obviously not that tobacco is bad for you!

Anyway, Sweet Caporal's chief claim to fame is its connection with what is now considered the Holy Grail of baseball cards, the T206 Honus Wagner card. In the early 1900s, the American Tobacco Company ran an advertising campaign that involved inserting cards of major league baseball players into packs of its Sweet Caporal and Piedmont brand cigarettes. Sometime later, Pittsburgh Pirates Hall of Famer Honus Wagner requested that the company pull his card from the promotion, supposedly because he feared his endorsement of tobacco was sending the wrong message to kids. The company complied and the result was that relatively few Wagner cards made it into circulation. While it's not the rarest baseball card—some fifty are known to exist—it's certainly the most coveted. Today, T206 Wagner cards can fetch well over $100,000, with one having sold in 2001 for $1.25 million. Time to check your grandfather's attic!

CLOSER LOOK: On the stairs leading up to the Building & Loan are the names of businesses officed in the same building. *(0:08:53)* The list includes a jeweler, a veterinarian, an ear, nose, and throat doctor, and a collection service. Also, just to the right of the stairs is a women's department store called Anderson's. The Building & Loan is located directly above Anderson's.

EXPLANATION REQUIRED: When George shows up at the office, Uncle Billy shouts, "Avast there, Captain Cook!" as he tries to prevent George from interrupting his father's meeting with Potter. *Avast* is an old nautical term meaning "stop" or "desist." Uncle Billy also uses the "Captain Cook" moniker years later on the day that George prepares for his overseas trip.

JUST WONDERING: Now if you're a Building & Loan shareholder and you see Billy Bailey running around every day with strings tied around his fingers to remind him of his daily duties, wouldn't that make you just the slightest bit uneasy? *(9:17)* Sure, today he just forgot to call the bank examiner, but what will it be tomorrow? Misplacing Building & Loan shareholder funds?

DID YOU KNOW? Are you clued in to the fact that the two employees at the Building & Loan are actually George's cousins? If not, don't feel bad; this familial tie is revealed only through the film's final script. Their names are Tilly (short for Matilda) and Eustace Bailey. Tilly and Eustace's desk nameplates confirm that they are both "Baileys." Look for Tilly's nameplate later in the film, just after George vaults over the counter during the bank run *(0:53:08)*, and Eustace's as George searches the office vault on Christmas Eve after Uncle Billy loses the deposit *(1:22:58)*.

We know that Tilly and Eustace are not Uncle Billy's children because they refer to him as "Uncle Billy." So they must be the children of an undisclosed brother of Peter and Billy Bailey. As for Tilly and Eustace's responsibilities at the Building & Loan, the final script identifies Tilly as a telephone operator and Eustace as an office clerk.

CAST ANECDOTES: Mary Treen and Charles Williams, who play cousins Tilly and Eustace, were B-movie regulars, each with over ninety films to their credit by the time they appeared in *It's a Wonderful Life* (Treen racked up some twenty-two in 1935 alone). Both were cast in familiar roles in *It's a Wonderful Life*. Treen typically played "plain Jane" nurses, phone operators, waitresses, and secretaries, while Williams was at home playing quirky, bespectacled clerks, photographers, and reporters.

Later in her career, Treen made several special guest appearances on television sitcoms, including *The Andy Griffith Show*, *Happy Days*, and *The Brady Bunch* (*Brady Bunch* fans will remember her as "Kay," Alice's killjoy replacement when Alice quits after a falling-out with the kids). Williams can be found in the Shirley Temple film *Just Around the Corner* (1938), as well as *The Thin Man* (1934, the first in the popular *Thin Man* film series) and *The Pride of the Yankees* (1942).

EXPLANATION REQUIRED: Listen closely here for two lines of "bonus" dialogue just after Peter Bailey closes the door behind young George. Returning to the argument at hand, Mr. Potter asks, "Well, what's the answer?" Peter Bailey responds, "Mr. Potter, you just humiliated me in front of my son." Well, there's no doubt about that. If only we could hear Potter's retort—it must have been a real zinger.

FILM ANECDOTES: Prior to filming, the script called for the scene to continue on after young George got kicked out of his dad's office. In it George considers seeking help from Uncle Billy with his drugstore dilemma, but Uncle Billy is in his office on the phone desperately trying to fend off a demanding bank examiner. (Remember, just before George sneaks into his dad's office Uncle Billy gets a call from the bank examiner.) While on the phone Uncle Billy lights a cigar and carelessly throws the match into the wastebasket.

Meanwhile, George finds Eustace frantically preparing figures for the bank examiner and Tilly on the phone with her friend Martha explaining, "Potter's here, the bank examiner's coming. It's a day of judgment." As George starts to interrupt Tilly, Uncle Billy yells for help from his office. There's now a fire in the wastebasket and Tilly comes to the rescue, dousing the flames with a pot of coffee. Seeing this mayhem, George decides he's better off solving this problem on his own.

Now this is one omitted scene that we would like to have seen. Plus, if it *had* been included, we would have known that Tilly and Eustace are George's cousins. The script, you see, called for George to refer to them as "Cousin Tilly" and "Cousin Eustace" when he asked them for help.

George Returns to the Store (0:10:26)

RANDOM THOUGHTS: When George returns from his dad's office, Mary is still at the counter working on her scoop of ice cream, even though Mr. Gower says that George left the store to deliver the capsules over an hour ago. Is this another film gaffe? That depends on whether or not you believe that Mr. Gower, in his drunken stupor, has lost track of time!

MUSIC NOTES: The original musical score written by Dimitri Tiomkin included two cues for the drugstore scenes, which Tiomkin titled *Death Telegram* and *Gower's Deliverance*. However, director Frank Capra omitted these cues from the final version, electing instead to have the scenes run sans music.

This change, and a slew of others, led to a falling out between the two men. Prior to *It's a Wonderful Life* Capra and Tiomkin had been best of friends, having collaborated on some of Capra's most successful films. Tiomkin, it seems, was accustomed to having his artistic judgment carry the day, and was quite perturbed when Capra treated his score cues as if they were mere suggestions. Indeed, several of Tiomkin's cues were cut whole-sale, while others were pared down, moved, or toned down. Capra added insult to injury by using cues from other films written by other composers. In his autobiography, *Please Don't Hate Me*, Tiomkin described Capra's handling of the score as "an all around scissors job."

Despite Tiomkin's displeasure (he did not speak with Capra for quite some time and never worked with him again), in the end Capra's decisions proved sound. There is little doubt that the drugstore scenes, as with other scenes where cues were omitted, work better without heavy, dramatic music.

To see how the rest of Tiomkin's original cues were treated, and for a complete rundown of the popular songs used in the film, be sure to check out the Musical Score section in the back of the guide.

FILM ANECDOTES: The name of Bedford Falls' resident druggist is a Capra touch. Columbia Pictures, Capra's employer during the 1930s, was for many years located on Gower Street. It also seems that a favorite hangout of studio employees was a drugstore located on said Gower Street.

CAST ANECDOTES: The actor who plays young George, Bobbie Anderson, delivers a solid performance, particularly in the dramatic backroom scenes at Gower Drugs. But for sheer notoriety, he's at the wrong end of the picture—the actors playing George and Mary's children all get to participate in the high-profile Christmas Eve scenes at the end of the film. Just an unavoidable downside to taking on the "early years" role, we suppose.

Another standout film on Anderson's resume is *The Bishop's Wife*, which was a Best Picture nominee just one year after *It's a Wonderful Life*. Somewhat improbably, that film is also a Christmas story that centers around a wingless angel (Cary Grant) sent down to earth to straighten things out. In his only scene, Anderson gets tagged in the face with a snowball thrown by none other than Karolyn Grimes, who played his daughter Zuzu (technically speaking) in *It's a Wonderful Life*.

2

GEORGE PREPARES TO "SEE THE WORLD"

"This business of nickels and dimes and spending all your life trying to figure out how to save three cents on a length of pipe . . . I'd go crazy. I want to do something big and something important. **"**
—GEORGE BAILEY

Still in flashback mode, we now go forward to June 1928 where we find George on the eve of an overseas excursion that he has been dreaming of since he was a young lad. George has apparently been working at the Building & Loan since graduating from high school. With his younger brother, Harry, now graduating, George has arranged for Harry to take over for him at the Building & Loan so that he can finally get a crack at college. But first, George intends to "see the world."

This rather extraordinary day in George's life starts off normally enough with George picking up a suitcase, a gift from Mr. Gower, at the luggage store. His new suitcase in hand, George makes his way through downtown Bedford Falls. Along the way George runs into several people we'll be seeing more of down the road, including his Uncle Billy, his cousins Eustace and Tilly, Bert the cop, Ernie the taxi driver, and the now decidedly grown-up Violet Bick. Bert, Ernie, and George take a brief time out to admire Violet's, um, dress, before George heads home to prepare for his trip.

Later that evening, we find George at home, about to sit down for his last meal at the old Bailey boarding house before the big trip. Meanwhile, Harry is getting ready for his high school graduation dance. After George and Harry engage in some good-natured shenanigans with their parents and Annie, the family maid, George and his dad sit down for a heart-to-heart talk.

Pop has some misgivings about Harry taking over for George, but George is adamant that he be allowed to pursue higher education.

As father and son discuss the Building & Loan's future, Harry heads out the door for the graduation dance. But before he goes he urges a reluctant George to drop by and join in on the festivities as there will be "lots of pretty girls." Let's hope George listens because one of those pretty girls might just be his future wife.

The Luggage Store *(0:11:40)*

HISTORY LESSON: George explains to the luggage store owner that he needs room on his suitcase for labels from all of the places he will visit, and mentions three places by name: Italy, Baghdad, and Samarkand. Whoa! This is no ordinary itinerary George has put together. Italy and Iraq are not exactly next door to each other. And in case you have no clue where or what Samarkand is, it's a city in present-day Uzbekistan, located some 150 miles north of Afghanistan. Uzbekistan spent a good part of the twentieth century as a socialist republic of the Soviet Union, until it finally gained independence in 1991.

George was probably attracted to Samarkand by its rich culture and history, which has led writers and historians to dub it "the Rome of the East." Samarkand's cultural origin is diverse to say the least, grounded in a mixture of Iranian, Indian, Persian, and Mongolian cultures. Its location on the Silk Road, the ancient trading route that linked China with Eastern and Western Europe, thickened the cultural mix.

Samarkand also passed through the hands of a rather eclectic list of conquerors. Alexander the Great kicked things off when he rolled into town in 329 B.C. Since then the city has been controlled by, among others, the Arabs, the Turks, Mongolian nomads, Genghis Khan, the empire of Timur (Tamerlane declared Samarkand "the capital of the world"), the Khanate of Bukhara, and the Russian Empire. How's that for cultural diversity?

RANDOM THOUGHTS: Piecing together George's travel itinerary from his comments, George would have had his work cut out for him if he was going to make it home in time for the start of college. After a 3,500-mile boat ride across the Atlantic (presumably to England), George would have traveled some 1,500 miles across Western Europe to two destinations that he mentions to Mary after the graduation dance, Rome and Athens. From there, it's another 1,500 miles or so across Turkey to the capital of Iraq—Baghdad. Then it's *another* 1,500 miles to Samarkand—via Tehran, Iran, and Ashgabat, Turkmenistan, where he would probably have caught the Trans-Caspian Railroad.

Of course, once he got to Samarkand, he would have to get back. Assuming he took in a few other sites along the way, George had signed up to travel over 17,000 miles in a mere ninety days, all by boat, rail, and dusty road. Incidentally, for Samarkand and other Central Asian destinations, George would have been well advised to have his travel papers in order. By 1928 the Soviet Union had already seized Samarkand and much of the surrounding region while creating the socialist republics of Uzbekistan and Turkmenistan.

CLOSER LOOK: The name of the luggage store, World Luggage and Sporting Goods Store, appears on the store's front door. The signage on the store's front window reads, "Boston Co. Suit Cases and Bags—Sporting Goods." Also, on the side window by the door, the store advertises "Ammunition."

DID YOU KNOW? George tells the luggage salesman that he's traveling to Europe by "cattle boat." George didn't have much choice but to get to Europe by boat—regular transatlantic airplane service did not begin until 1939—but a cattle boat would have made for some rough going. Cattle boats were, in fact, used for transporting livestock between North America and Europe. But they also served as a cheap way for humans (particularly immigrants) to get across the Atlantic. While the accommodations may have been luxurious from a cow's perspective, they were decidedly not so for the human cargo.

George Thanks Mr. Gower *(0:12:59)*

CLOSER LOOK: The contraption that George uses to make his wish for "a million dollars" is an old-fashioned cigar lighter. And while we're hanging out at the tobacco counter, here are some tobacco-related advertisements to look for as George and Mr. Gower exchange pleasantries: Sir Walter Raleigh Smoking Tobacco, Old Glory Rum Cured Cigarette Holders, Beuscher's Missouri Hickory Pipes, and Scotch Snuff.

RANDOM THOUGHTS: George promised Mr. Gower that he wouldn't tell a soul about the poison capsules mishap, and given that Mr. Gower is still in business some nine years later, George appears to have been true to his word. But let's hope George got more than a lousy suitcase out of the deal, like, say, lifetime dibs at the drugstore's soda fountain.

A Walk Through Downtown Bedford Falls *(0:13:13)*

FILM ANECDOTES: As Uncle Billy, Eustace, and Tilly yell to George from a Building & Loan window, check out the pigeons to the right of the window. *(0:13:15)* The set designers actually kept pigeons and other animals on the set to give Bedford Falls a more realistic look and feel.

CLOSER LOOK: In the same scene, look for the street signs that appear beneath the window. *(0:13:15)* The signs tell us that the Building & Loan is located on the corner of Genesee Street (it's actually a boulevard) and Jefferson Avenue. Genesee Street serves as the main road through downtown Bedford Falls. The Building & Loan offices are on the second floor (above Anderson's), with windows fronting on both Genesee Street and Jefferson Avenue.

EXPLANATION REQUIRED: We're still scratching our heads trying to figure out why Bedford Falls' main street is named Genesee Street. Whoever selected the street's name for the film undoubtedly knew that it had roots in New York State, which is where Bedford Falls is located. *Genesee* is a Seneca Indian word meaning roughly "beautiful valley," and the Seneca Indians lived in what is now western New York, where the aptly named Genesee River runs. While we appreciate the New York tie-in, it still strikes us as odd that Bedford Falls, which is itself a river town, would adopt the name of a different river from a different part of New York as the name for its main street.

HISTORY LESSON: As George greets his pals Bert the cop and Ernie the taxi driver, Bert is holding a newspaper with a headline reading SMITH WINS NOMINATION! *(0:13:24)* Most people assume that this headline is an inside joke referring to Jimmy Stewart's leading role in the film *Mr. Smith Goes to Washington*, a theory that seems even more plausible given that Frank Capra directed that film as well.

In fact, the headline refers to an actual event in American political history, albeit an obscure one. In late June 1928, the Democrats held their national convention in Houston, Texas, at which Alfred E. Smith won the Democratic Party's nomination for president. The headline references Smith's victory, which would have been of particular interest to Bedford Fallsians given that by 1928 he had served four terms as governor of New York.

Smith's nomination was historically noteworthy because he was the first person of Irish heritage to be nominated for president by a major political party. His Republican opponent, Herbert Hoover, launched a nasty little campaign, playing the religious bigotry card and casting Smith as morally unfit for office given his support for the repeal of Prohibition (they dubbed him "Al-coholic Smith"). The tactics paid off as Hoover won in a landslide. But Smith seemed to have the last laugh as the Hoover administration was tagged with responsibility for the Great Depression, and Prohibition was repealed anyway in 1933.

CLOSER LOOK: A rather involved film gaffe occurs in the vignette when George, Bert, and Ernie ogle Violet as she saunters down the street. Two separate shots show the guys slack jawed by Ernie's taxi. Watch as the same woman—wearing a print dress and holding the brim of her hat with her right hand—walks past the taxi in both shots. *(0:13:51; 0:13:59)*

But hold on a minute here. Is there more to this gaffe than first meets the eye? Let's back up a bit to when George first approaches Bert and Ernie. In the very first shot, look in the background for a familiar sight—a woman walking down the sidewalk in a print dress and holding the brim of her hat with her right hand. *(0:13:25)* Then, in the next shot of Ernie in the driver's seat of his cab, there she is again, holding that same hat! *(0:13:32)* This is getting weird.

And just when you think you've got your arms around this gaffe, the film cuts to Violet on the sidewalk, and guess who is walking a few paces behind her? You got it, the ubiquitous print-dress-wearing, hat-holding woman. *(0:13:35)* If you're keeping score at home, that's five walk-throughs by the same woman in the span of about thirty seconds. Obviously, on this particular day the director was running a little short on extras!

FILM ANECDOTES: One oft-heard bit of *It's a Wonderful Life* trivia is that Bert and Ernie of *Sesame Street* fame take their names from Bert the cop and Ernie the taxi driver. But the creators of the children's show characters apparently insist that this is not the case. Sure, it *could* be a coincidence, but forgive us for being skeptical.

CAST ANECDOTES: Bert and Ernie were played by character actors Ward Bond and Frank Faylen. Bond was at his best playing gruff characters with a soft side. Among his more than 250 film credits are two other American classics, *Gone with the Wind* (1939, as Yankee Captain Tom) and *The Maltese Falcon* (1941, as Police Sergeant Polhaus). He appeared in several notable westerns, including *My Darling Clementine* (1946) and *Wagon Master* (1950), and his proficiency in playing cowpokes led to his landing the starring role in the 1950s television series *Wagon Train*. Ward was also best pals with John Wayne (they were football mates at USC) and the two appeared in a slew of films together.

By the time Faylen took on the role of Ernie, he had already appeared as a taxi driver in no less than six pictures, including *No Time for Comedy* (1940), starring Jimmy Stewart. His numerous portrayals of the trusty cabbie reportedly led a Los Angeles area taxi driver's union to make him an honorary member. Other notable Faylen film credits include *The Grapes of Wrath* (1940, also featuring Bond), *The Pride of the Yankees* (1942, as the Yankees' third-base coach, in which he shares a scene with Babe Ruth himself), *The Lost Weekend* (1945), *Road to Rio* (1947, with Bob Hope and Bing Crosby), and *Funny Girl* (1968, with Barbra Streisand).

George at Home with the Family *(0:14:16)*

MUSIC NOTES: Quick! Aside from the opening credits, when is the first time we hear *Buffalo Gals* in the film? The graduation dance? After the dance? Well, the song also shows up during this scene. Listen closely to George and Harry while they are upstairs (off screen) at the Bailey house getting ready for the evening—they can both be heard singing George and Mary's soon-to-be theme song. But if we're being technical, the answer is May 1919 in Gower Drugs—young George is whistling a rough version of the tune just after he shows up for work.

CLOSER LOOK: Did you pick up on the fact that the Baileys have a pet? It's a French sheepdog, and though he has no name in the film, his real-life name was Shag. Where does Shag appear, you ask? Several places, actually. In this scene, he can be found first lurking near Ma Bailey as she calls the boys down for dinner. *(0:14:25)* He then scoots past the dining room table, and starts barking as George and Harry throw their mother into Mr. Bailey's lap.

In fact, Shag barks so much in this scene that Stewart appears to get fed up and comes out of character just long enough to tell Shag to "Shut up!" Shag also shows up in an earlier scene, running with young George and his pals as they head through downtown Bedford Falls. *(0:5:08)* Finally, Shag makes a cameo at George and Mary's wedding send-off, bounding down the front staircase just behind the newlyweds. *(0:50:16)*

JUST WONDERING: We learn during George's dinner conversation with his dad that Peter Bailey voluntarily appointed Potter to the Building & Loan's board of directors. What in the world was he thinking here? "Hmmm . . . let's see . . . Potter, my only competitor and most hated enemy, is making my life miserable, so what should I do to get him off my back? I know! I'll give him a seat on my own company's board of directors." Huh? Old man Bailey should hardly have been surprised when Potter later used his position to attempt to put the Building & Loan out of business. Perhaps Potter was on to something when he declared that Peter Bailey was not a businessman!

FILM ANECDOTES: So does Harry have a special talent for balancing pies on his head? Well, film lore has it that actor Todd Karns was actually aided by a concave pie tin and a few strategically placed fasteners. This sounds likely, but there's no way to tell from watching the film. What is clear is that, with or without aid, Karns is definitely struggling to keep that pie on his head as he exchanges lines with Stewart. So we would not be surprised if a few pies were lost in capturing this scene.

CAST ANECDOTES: Serving up some well-timed one-liners in this scene is the Bailey's sassy yet good-natured family housekeeper, Annie. Actress Lillian Randolph's voice and face would have been quite familiar to movie audiences back in 1946, having previously played Birdie the family housekeeper in the wildly popular *The Great Gildersleeve* radio show (debuting in 1941) and film series (beginning in 1942).

EXPLANATION REQUIRED: It's a little tough to catch on the first go-around, but the question that George asks Harry as he walks through the dining room with his hands full of pies is "Got a match?" Thank goodness Harry doesn't fall for this old gag—dropping one of Annie's homemade pies surely would have earned him a swat or two from her broom.

JUST WONDERING: What will be Harry's alcoholic beverage of choice this evening? As Harry is leaving for the dance, his dad admonishes him not to drink any *gin* tonight. Harry briefly protests, but then gives up, no doubt because he's savvy enough to realize that his dad's rule has a loophole big enough to drive a beer truck through. Basically, Harry can drink any type of booze he pleases, just as long as it's not gin!

CLOSER LOOK: Look for the framed butterfly collection hanging in Mr. and Mrs. Bailey's dining room. Later in the film we discover that George inherits the framings as they both appear in George and Mary's house some seventeen years later during the Christmas Eve scene (just to the right of the Christmas tree). *(1:25:19)*

CAST ANECDOTES: Playing George's honest, hardworking father and doting mother are Samuel Hinds and Beulah Bondi; both are perfect fits for their roles. Hinds could convey the wise old soul with the best of them, which makes sense considering he graduated from Harvard and had a law degree. He also would have had the inside track on the role of Peter Bailey, having previously worked for Capra in *You Can't Take It with You.* To see Hinds in a less genteel role, watch *Destry Rides Again* (1939), a hoot of a western starring Jimmy Stewart where Hinds plays a delightfully crooked mayor.

Bondi was at home playing kind-hearted matronly types, but was equally skilled at playing the mean, nasty ones. So it was her good fortune that *It's a Wonderful Life* made use of a plot device that allowed her to play both types in the same film. Bondi was cinch for the role of Ma Bailey as she had already played Jimmy Stewart's mother in four films: *The Gorgeous Hussy* (1936, though with no scenes together), *Of Human Hearts* (1938, nominated for Best Supporting Actress), *Vivacious Lady* (1938), and *Mr. Smith Goes to Washington* (1939). If you want to see more of Bondi at her devilish best, track down *Shepard of the Hills* (1941), where she plays a wicked aunt.

One film that is not on Bondi's resume, but should be, is *The Grapes of Wrath.* Bondi lobbied hard for the role of Ma Joad, even going so far as to make camp with some Depression-battered Okies to better understand their plight; but all to no avail. Watch this film and you'll see why Bondi's knack for realism and avoiding oversentimentality would have served the part well.

3

THE HIGH SCHOOL GRADUATION DANCE

❝ What is it you want, Mary? What do you want?
You want the moon? Just say the word and I'll
throw a lasso around it and pull it down. Hey,
that's a pretty good idea, Mary. I'll give you the
moon, Mary. **❞**

—GEORGE BAILEY

W e now come to a gem of a scene—the high school graduation dance.
Remember, it's Harry Bailey and Mary Hatch's graduation, both of
whom are four years George's junior. Although George and a few of his pals
(namely Sam Wainwright and Marty Hatch) are crashing the dance, no one
seems to mind. George soon finds himself dancing with the resplendent
Mary Hatch, and it's pretty obvious that she is just as enamored with
George now as when she was a little girl hanging around the soda fountain
at Gower Drugs. But the dance comes at a price—George, it seems, has
"stolen" his dance with Mary from another boy, who soon seeks revenge by
activating the newly installed retractable gym floor resting over the pool.
The teenage rascal's plan works to perfection, and with a throng of amused
dancegoers looking on, George and Mary "Charleston" ever closer to the
edge of the parting gym floor before taking a most unexpected plunge.

George and Mary walk home from the dance under the light of a full
moon, having traded in their wet clothes for a robe and an ill-fitting football
uniform. By now these two are in full flirtation mode. They share a song.
They exchange wishes by throwing rocks at the old Granville house. George,
feeling quite amorous, promises to "lasso the moon" for Mary, and then

shares some deep metaphysical thoughts about moons being swallowed and moonbeams shooting from fingers and toes and such.

But there seems to be more smoke than fire here; at least that's what a grumpy neighbor thinks who has been privy to their coquetry and is convinced that George will never get around to the real task at hand—planting one on Mary. Before George can prove the neighbor wrong, the clumsy lout steps on Mary's robe and forces her to take cover in a nearby bush, sans clothing.

As George contemplates how to best capitalize on his good fortune, the evening takes a tragic turn. (Get used to the emotional roller coaster—we'll be seeing this pattern of juxtaposed emotional highs and lows several more times before this one's over.) Harry and Uncle Billy arrive on the scene with news that George's father has suffered a stroke. With that, George and Mary's magical evening together comes to an end.

The Graduation Dance (0:19:00)

CLOSER LOOK: Notice how much older Jimmy Stewart looks compared to the other kids at the dance. While Donna Reed was a still plausible twenty-five years old at the time the scene was filmed, Stewart was thirty-eight, a full sixteen years older than the character he was playing.

MUSIC NOTES: The first tune heard playing at the dance is a catchy little number called "Collegiate," which was among the top hits of 1925. As with the "Charleston," the song had an accompanying dance that was all the rage among the raccoon coat–wearing crowd. Filled with cheeky lines about those heady college campus days of the Roaring Twenties (*C'lle-giate. C'lle-giate. Yes! We are col-le-giate./ No-thing in-ter-med-jate. Noooo Ma'am./ Trou-sers, bag-gy. And our clothes look raggy*), the song will have you reaching for your skimmer hat and ukelele in no time.

EXPLANATION REQUIRED: During this scene, Marty Hatch asks George whether he remembers his younger sister Mary. This prompts Sam Wainwright to jokingly chime in, "Mamma wants you, Marty! Mamma wants you!" The group has a knowing laugh at Sam's imitation. But if the line leaves you wondering whether you missed something, there's a good reason.

The film's opening sledding scene originally included a young Mary nagging her brother to come home just before the accident, yelling, "Mamma wants you, Marty! Mamma wants you!" However, after some last-minute script changes young Mary was cut from the scene. Unfortunately, the graduation dance scenes—including the one with Sam mimicking young Mary—were shot *before* the sledding scene. Thus, cutting Mary's part from the sledding scene left Sam's line dangling without any context. This is a textbook example of why it's not such a good idea to make major script changes on the fly.

DID YOU KNOW? Mary, Violet, and the rest of the girls at the dance make use of dance cards. Violet flashes her card as she talks with George *(0:19:57)*, while Mary's card can be seen on her wrist as she dances the "Charleston" *(0:21:44)*. Back in the 1920s, dance cards were commonplace at high school dances and provided a fun way for dancegoers to keep track of their dance partners for the evening. Here's how they worked. The dance card (or booklet) listed the evening's dance program, and had a space next to each dance

for entering one's dance partners. Boys solicited dances from the girls, and the girls either accepted or declined. Once a girl said yes and entered a boy in her card she was not supposed to back out of the deal.

Here, Violet and Mary have a lot to learn about dance card etiquette. First, Violet announces to George, Marty, and Sam that she has a "third of a dance" left. While this is no doubt a creative way to increase your exposure to the boys, penciling in more than one dance partner for a single song is plain old bad form. Violet then asks George, "What am I bid?" This is an auctioneer's term that means "How much will you pay for this item?" Auctioning off dances to the highest bidder? Also bad form.

As for Mary, she commits a dance card faux pas by allowing George to cut in on her scheduled dance partner. But perhaps Mary can be forgiven for this solecism since she is, after all, simply seeking to dance with her destiny.

CAST ANECDOTES: If you can believe it, the freckle-faced mope who corners Mary on the dance floor is none other than Carl "Alfalfa" Switzer of *Our Gang/Little Rascals* fame. Born on August 7, 1927, in Paris, Illinois, Switzer enjoyed huge success as a child actor, making dozens of *Our Gang* comedy shorts between 1935 and 1940. In the 1950s the shorts were repackaged for television as *The Little Rascals*, but neither Switzer nor any of the other *Our Gang* members shared in the financial gains brought about through syndication.

The gangly Switzer was eighteen when he appeared in *It's a Wonderful Life*. While his career in feature films consisted largely of bit parts and small supporting roles, he did appear in some pretty high-profile films, including: *The High and Mighty* (1954, with John Wayne), *Going My Way* (1944, with Bing Crosby), *Pat and Mike* (1952, with Spencer Tracy and Katherine Hepburn), and *The Defiant Ones* (1958, with Tony Curtis and Sidney Poitier). To make ends meet, Switzer tended bar and, of all things, guided bear hunts. On January 21, 1959, at the age of thirty-one, Switzer was shot dead by an aquaintence after a drunken Switzer confronted him over a fifty-dollar debt. The man somehow walked based on a rather dubious story that he had acted in self-defense after Switzer came at him with a knife.

The Big Charleston Contest *(0:21:11)*

EXPLANATION REQUIRED: In announcing the Charleston contest, Harry states, "Oyez, oyez, oyez! The big Charleston contest!" *Oyez* basically means "hear ye" and is typically used by an officer of the court to call a courtroom to order, as in "Oyez, oyez, oyez! The court is now in session!"

CLOSER LOOK: The band playing at the dance is Bedford High's very own—you can just make out the high school's name on the face of the band's drum set. *(0:21:29)*

CLOSER LOOK: During the Charleston contest, look for the boy whose tuxedo bib unexpectedly rolls up on him while he's dancing. *(0:22:00)* Why do these things always happen to the fat kid?

EXPLANATION REQUIRED: As Sam and Violet set their sights on winning the loving cup, the school's principal, Mr. Partridge, taps Violet on the shoulder. At first blush it appears that he's acting as a judge and eliminating the couple from the contest. But recall that Harry announces that couples *not tapped* by the judges are to remain on the floor. And rather than clearing the floor, Violet and Sam keep dancing.

So what gives here? We think that Mr. Partridge is assuming the role of a chaperone and is good-naturedly letting Violet know that she's showing a little too much leg as she swivels. Look for Mr. Partridge gesturing to Violet's hemline, just before she pauses to give Mr. Partridge an apologetic hug.

JUST WONDERING: With Violet and Sam hitting it off so well on the dance floor, don't you think it's a shame that they don't end up together? We think they would have been a perfect match: Sam was destined to make a fortune, and Violet, with her extravagant tastes, would have been a natural at spending that fortune.

CLOSER LOOK: Notice anything different about Violet's appearance compared to the other girls at the dance? How about the fact that Violet is the only girl wearing a black dress? Here, director Frank Capra appears to have resorted to some subliminal messaging to convey the notion that Violet is a "bad girl." As if that was really necessary.

EXPLANATION REQUIRED: As George and Mary dance the Charleston, a brooding Freddie is approached by another boy, Mickey, who has seen George cut in on Freddie's dance with Mary. Mickey asks Freddie, "What's the matter, Othello? Jealous?" For those of you not up on your Shakespeare, this is a reference to the play *Othello*. The story, as you might suspect, is one of jealousy. Othello is duped into believing that his wife has been unfaithful to him. In a jealous rage, Othello kills her, and at the same time seeks to do away with her suspected lover. Thankfully, life does not imitate art at the graduation dance, and Freddie is content with paying back George and Mary through a harmless prank.

MUSIC NOTES: While George and Mary's song may be "Buffalo Gals," it's actually the "Charleston" that seals their fate. How could they not end up together after performing such an unforgettable aquatic rendition of the dance? Derived from an African American folk dance, the Charleston swept the country in the mid-1920s and remained hugely popular for the rest of the decade. The original version of the dance was considered so wild in nature that some ballrooms either banned it or displayed signs admonishing dancers to "Please Charleston Quietly." Obviously, no such sign was posted in the Bedford Falls High School gym!

FILM ANECDOTES: If a retractable gym floor seems a bit implausible to you, think again. This scene was filmed at Beverly Hills High School, which in 1940 installed a gym floor above its pool as a space-saving measure. Called the "Swim-Gym," the facility remains fully functional today. In the film, a basketball backboard is located behind the band *(0:21:17)*, and you can just make out the center-court markings of the basketball court as the floor begins to spread *(0:23:02)*.

With its full-arched roof and skylights, the Swim-Gym has the look and feel of an old airplane hangar. Happily, sixty years after filming the place hasn't changed much—even the courtside "well," where Freddie and Mickey conspire to open the floor, is still there. The one surprise, though, is its size. Though the Swim-Gym looks positively cavernous in the film, it's actually pretty cozy, with just enough room for six or so rows of bench seats around the perimeter of the court/pool.

CLOSER LOOK: The pool scene is best described as organized chaos. The film's budget indicates that the director hired several life guards for the scene, and with good reason. There's not much room to land and everyone is basically jumping on top of each other. There is some method to the madness, though. As extras jump in, most get out of harm's way by swimming underneath the gym floor. The head-first dives that some of the male extras perform would seem to be a bad call as the depth marker on the far side of the pool indicates that the pool is only 5' 9" where the floor splits. *(0:23:37)*

Look for Freddie and Mickey actually jumping *twice*, first in a medium shot *(0:23:41)*, and then again a few seconds later in a long shot of the very same action *(0:23:49)*. This doubling up on scene footage is understandable given that the scene was undoubtedly a "one taker." Look also for Stewart and Reed's stunt doubles as they try to swim out of the way with extras diving in from all sides. *(0:23:35)* Stewart's double is particularly noticeable as he does not appear to have much hair on his head!

RANDOM THOUGHTS: We never learn the Bedford Falls High School mascot or nickname, but given that Bedford Falls is a river town, our vote is for the Mighty River Rats.

Walking Mary Home *(00:24:03)*

CLOSER LOOK: The name "B. C. Berkley" appears on a mailbox that George and Mary walk past in this scene. *(0:24:50)* We were hoping to stumble upon a story to go along with the use of this name, but so far we've got nothing. If you figure this one out, by all means let us know.

CLOSER LOOK: As George and Mary flirt their way down the sidewalk, keep an eye and ear out for a single line of dubbed dialogue. Mary playfully tries to coax George into saying, rather more directly, that she's the prettiest girl in town. George replies, "I don't know, maybe I will say it." But on film it's clear that George is not saying it at all.

RANDOM THOUGHTS: George doesn't think much of the old Granville house, declaring that he wouldn't even live in it if he were a ghost. But we respectfully disagree. In addition to its ruinous condition, the house's architectural style is perfect for a haunted house.

The style is known as Second Empire, an ornate French style that was quite popular in America in the 1870s. The telltale feature of this style is the mansard roof—basically a two-sloped roof, with a steep lower slope and a near-horizontal upper slope (picture the house in *Psycho*). *(0:25:47)* Our theory on why houses with mansard roofs are so creepy is that they create the impression that something untoward is happening up in the attic. Hey, whatever did happen to the Granvilles, anyway?

RANDOM THOUGHTS: George and Mary take turns making wishes by throwing rocks at the Granville house windows. Now the cardinal rule of wish-making is that you're not supposed to tell anyone what you just wished for; else the wish won't come true, right? Wise to this, Mary refuses to tell George her wish, revealing it only on their wedding night *after* it had come true. George, on the other hand, just can't help himself and blurts out his wish mere seconds after making it. And just like that, George's fate is sealed: instead of a life filled with adventures in Italy and Greece, George will be keeping the Granville ghosts company for decades to come.

CLOSER LOOK: Another newspaper headline appears during this scene, but this one is a challenge to read. As George and Mary flirt, a grumpy neighbor watches them with disdain from his porch, annoyed that they have interrupted his reading of the newspaper. In the first shot of the neighbor, the headline of his newspaper reads REPUBLICAN CHIEFS HAIL MAINE AS SIGN OF HOOVER VICTORY. *(0:26:03)* In those days, Maine was widely viewed in American politics as the bellwether state for election outcomes. The oft-stated axiom was "As Maine goes, so goes the nation." The headline therefore fits somewhat plausibly with actual events taking place in the 1928 presidential campaign, which pitted Herbert Hoover against Alfred E. Smith.

CLOSER LOOK: At the top of our list of random and obscure scene details is the fact that for some reason the grumpy neighbor is wearing not one, but two undershirts. A fashion trend of bygone days? Maybe, but more likely the neighbor's layered look is attributable to a chilly night on the set. While the scene has the look and feel of a stage set, it was actually filmed outdoors on a studio back lot. This also explains why we can see Reed and Stewart's breath a couple of times during the scene. *(0:24:13; 0:26:58)* Whatever the reason, you now have another item of supreme intrigue to look out for in years to come.

CLOSER LOOK: Our grumpy neighbor is also the source of a couple of film gaffes. Recall that earlier that same day George runs into Bert, who is holding a newspaper with the headline SMITH WINS NOMINATION! Unless the neighbor is reading the evening edition, he should have a paper with the same headline as Bert's. And any doubt as to whether this is a true gaffe is removed in the next scene when George addresses the Building & Loan's board of directors. Although that scene is set a full three months after the night of the graduation dance, Tilly Bailey is shown holding a newspaper with the very same REPUBLICAN CHIEFS HAIL . . . headline. *(0:34:24)*

The other gaffe appears in the third shot of the neighbor, when the newspaper's masthead reads "Los Angeles," as in the *Los Angeles Times*, as in the real-life local newspaper where these scenes were filmed. *(0:27:05)* We can only surmise that the actor playing the grumpy neighbor (Dick Elliott) just got tired of reading a fake newspaper and wanted to catch up on the day's news.

FILM ANECDOTES: Film lore has is it that Donna Reed, an Iowa farm girl, had a pretty good arm and actually broke the window of the Granville house with her throw. Well, there's no doubt she has an impressive throwing motion; but the timing of the glass breaking is just a hair off, so we are leaning more toward myth than reality. Indeed, to our eye it's more likely that *Stewart's* throw was legitimate.

DID YOU KNOW? This scene contains two items of horticultural interest. First, the tall, slender, flowered stalks along the fence line are hollyhocks. Later on, look for Ruth Dakin Bailey brandishing a hollyhock stalk as the Bailey clan poses for a picture on Mrs. Bailey's front porch. *(0:37:47)* Second, after losing her robe, Mary hides in the middle of a hydrangea bush.

Director Frank Capra later insisted that the hydrangea bush—and all other foliage in the film—was real, but we're not convinced. To us not only does the bush look fake, but it also *sounds* fake. And when Mary gives the bush a good shake, a flowered clump falls to the ground—not what you'd expect with a real bush. Whatever the case, to our eye the bush most closely resembles a rather sad version of a "mophead" hydrangea known as *Hydrangea arborescens* "Grandiflora."

JUST WONDERING: What exactly is the mischievous "deal" that George has in mind when he negotiates with Mary for the return of her robe? Wherever your imagination takes you, rest assured that the deal was not going to be "I'll give you back your robe if you promise to marry me."

CAST ANECDOTES: For both Donna Reed and Jimmy Stewart, getting from small-town America to Tinseltown was no small trick. Upon graduating from high school in 1938, Reed was all but headed for college in the Midwest when her aunt offered her a place to stay in Los Angeles. Reed seized the opportunity and was initially intent on pursuing a career in radio broadcasting. Before long, Reed landed in the drama department at Los Angeles City College. Although she had done some acting in her high school days, she was by no means a standout in her stage classes.

Then in December 1940 she caught a huge break. At the college's "Queen's Ball" she was voted most beautiful coed, and the next day the *Los Angeles Times* carried the news along with a fetching photograph of her. Studio executives took notice, realizing that her fresh, wholesome features would transfer nicely onto the silver screen. Within a few months Reed inked a modest deal with MGM, and by the end of 1941 she had already appeared in four films, the most prominent of which was the fourth installment in the popular *Thin Man* series, *Shadow of the Thin Man*.

When Stewart graduated from high school in 1928, he had no ambitions of becoming an actor. Instead, he enrolled at Princeton University and pursued a degree in, of all things, architecture—wouldn't George Bailey have been jealous! While Stewart was set on a career as a builder, the dearth of construction during the Great Depression forced him to reconsider. Meanwhile, Stewart's ability to play the accordion landed him a spot in a renowned performing arts group headed by some of his Princeton mates. Stewart soon found himself acting in Broadway plays, and after a string of well-received theatrical performances, MGM took notice and called Stewart in for a screen test. By the summer of 1935, Stewart had a contract with MGM and was cast in the role of a young go-getting reporter in a film called *The Murder Man*, starring Spencer Tracy.

4

GEORGE'S PLAN TO "SEE THE WORLD" GETS DERAILED

❝ This town needs this measly one-horse institution if only to have some place where people can come without crawling to Potter. **❞**

—GEORGE BAILEY

In the next sequence, twice George finds himself on the brink of escaping the town and business he loves to hate, only to have circumstances cruelly conspire to keep him put. First we learn that George's father has, in fact, passed away after suffering a stroke on the night of the graduation dance. Foregoing the obligatory deathbed scene, the film skips ahead three months to a meeting of the Building & Loan's board of directors. At the meeting the board pays its respects to Peter Bailey and his work, and then sets out to appoint his successor.

But Potter, himself a board member, has his own agenda and presents a surprise motion to the board to dissolve the Building & Loan. This sets off some fireworks in the room, with Uncle Billy nearly jumping across the table to get at Potter after one of his more venomous remarks. (George and Uncle Billy better get used to Potter's antics, though, as things are only going to get worse.) George counters with an impassioned speech on why Bedford Falls needs the Building & Loan. The board responds by rejecting Potter's motion, but there's a hitch. George must agree to assume his father's position as head of the Building & Loan, else the board will vote with Potter and liquidate the business.

We now skip ahead nearly four years to June 1932 for a watershed day in George's life. The day kicks off with George and Uncle Billy at the train station awaiting Harry's return from college. George, now around twenty-six, has begrudgingly spent the last four years running the Building & Loan. After his father's death, George gave his college tuition money to Harry with the understanding that upon graduating Harry would return to Bedford Falls and relieve George of his duties at the Building & Loan.

With Harry's impending return, George is convinced that his days in the backwaters of Bedford Falls are numbered. But just seconds after arriving Harry drops a couple of bombshells. Not only has he secretly married, but he's also all but decided to take a job offered to him by his new bride's father. The consequences of Harry's actions are painfully evident to George: he won't be going to college, he won't be "seeing the world" anytime soon, and he won't be ridding himself of this albatross of a family business.

Later that night, Mrs. Bailey hosts a party to celebrate both Harry's return from college and his new marriage. Not surprisingly, for George the occasion is bittersweet as it sinks in that he will remain cooped up in Bedford Falls for the foreseeable future. Sensing George's disappointment with the state of affairs, his mother tries at least to get his love life back on track by encouraging George to call on his one-time dance partner Mary Hatch, who has just returned from college.

But George is reluctant to do so since he knows that his old pal Sam Wainwright has been courting Mary. Instead, George wanders downtown, where he runs into the ever sultry Violet Bick. Violet sees this chance encounter as the perfect opportunity to finally snag the man who has eluded her all these years. But when she learns that George's idea of a good time is walking through the grass in his bare feet, the far less adventurous Violet sends George scurrying back off into the night, alone again.

George Addresses the Building & Loan Board *(0:29:47)*

CLOSER LOOK: At the board meeting George wears a black armband on the left sleeve of both his suit and his overcoat in memory of his father. A board member confirms that George's dad died a full three months ago, so it seems a little odd that George is still wearing an armband. But given the purpose of the board meeting—to appoint Peter Bailey's successor—and the fact that this may well be the first board meeting since Peter Bailey's death, we'll cut George some slack on this one.

JUST WONDERING: OK, this is the second time that Potter is shown in the offices of the Building & Loan, so now we have to ask: how has the wheelchair-bound Potter been getting up to the second floor of the Building & Loan all these years? Unless there's an elevator we don't know about or

Potter is able to negotiate stairs with assistance, then the only way Potter is getting up those stairs is via a "fireman's carry" courtesy of his goon. Wait, we're getting a visual here, and it's not pretty!

CAST ANECDOTES: That Potter appears in a wheelchair is no accident. Lionel Barrymore, who plays Potter, had been wheelchair-bound since the late 1930s as a result of severe arthritis. Lionel was part of the famed Barrymore family of actors; his brother John and sister Ethyl were also accomplished stage and film actors. Barrymore's film credits include *A Free Soul* (1931, for which he won his only Academy Award), *The Grand Hotel* (1932), *Camille* (1936), Capra's *You Can't Take It with You* (1938), and a slew of films in the ever-popular *Dr. Kildare* series. He was also an accomplished radio actor, best known for his annual portrayal of the Potteresque Scrooge in *A Christmas Carol*. By the way, in case you're wondering whether Lionel is related to actress Drew Barrymore, he is. Lionel's brother John is Drew Barrymore's grandfather, which makes Lionel her great-uncle.

RANDOM THOUGHTS: The scatterbrained Uncle Billy claims that he is fifty-five in this scene, but Tilly reminds him that he's actually fifty-six. Since this scene is set in 1928, that would make Uncle Billy a rather youthful-looking seventy-three at the end of the film.

George and Uncle Billy Greet Harry at the Station *(0:35:03)*

CLOSER LOOK: This scene begins with George and Uncle Billy talking before Harry's train arrives. The first audible line is George saying, "There are plenty of jobs for a man who likes to travel." But the two clearly exchange a few lines before this one. Unfortunately, these lines are obscured by Clarence and Joseph's voiceover. Fear not, though. We have reconstructed this "lost" dialogue with a little help from the script as it stood prior to filming. Referring to his desire for Harry to relieve him at the Building & Loan, George says, "He's going to take my job, and I'm gonna bolt like that," as he smacks his hands together. A more pragmatic Uncle Billy replies, "Have you heard of the Depression? Where you gonna find another job in these times?"

FILM ANECDOTES: We always assumed that the train station scene was shot on a studio back lot; but then it dawned on us—that is one big honkin' train! Sure enough, a little digging revealed that the scene was filmed on location at the now-defunct La Manda Park railroad depot in Pasadena, California. La Manda Park was a regular stop on the Santa Fe Railway line that ran between Los Angeles and San Bernadino. Until 1953 the depot stood at the intersection of what is now San Gabriel Boulevard and Walnut Street. Today, there's scarcely a trace of the old line in the area.

In the film you can see several coach cars and a baggage car, but for some reason Capra chose not to show the real attraction—the vintage 1921 steam engine that was pulling whole thing. Too bad, as it looked pretty darn cool. In fairness, Capra had to keep the shots for this scene fairly tight due to the presence of several palm trees on the depot grounds—palm trees simply would not do for a scene that is supposed to take place in New York. From what you *can* see of the depot, it appears just as it was, except for a few props and, of course, the depot's swapped-out station sign.

JUST WONDERING: Excuse us, but when did Harry become such a weasel? While he gave us hints of this aspect of his character on graduation night (planning to take his mom's china without permission), the stunt he pulls at the station is one for the ages. Not only does Harry flat out welsh on his promise to take over for George at the Building & Loan, he can't even muster up an apology for his older brother. Instead, all he does is blame his wife for "speaking out of turn." And after lamely excusing himself to fetch his bags, Harry will not be heard from again on the subject. Come on, Harry, get with it! You wouldn't even be *alive* if it wasn't for George.

RANDOM THOUGHTS: Well, thankfully, if anyone is capable of straightening Harry out, it's his new wife. From this scene alone it's clear that this girl's got a lot of moxie. First, with an air of casual confidence, Ruth corrects Harry on her new name. Then she good-naturedly mocks George's stiff greeting with an equally stiff and affected "How do you do?" Only then does George realize that a kiss—not a handshake—is in order for his new sister-in-law.

CAST ANECDOTES: The gorgeous Virginia Patton gives a refined performance as Ruth Dakin Bailey, but there's no denying that it's a pretty limited role. Basically one minute at the train station, a few seconds at the "welcome home" party, and that's it. She doesn't even get to participate in George and Mary's wedding send-off or the Christmas Eve festivities. We would have liked to have seen more of her, but at least she still managed to gain an always-coveted spot in the film's opening credits.

This film was a big break for Patton—before *It's a Wonderful Life* she had appeared in only a handful of films, largely uncredited. She did play the lead in her next film, *The Burning Cross* (1947), a film notable for tackling racial subject matter before its time. However, Patton retired from film after just a few more pictures.

By the way, Patton is one of the few adult members of the cast who (as of this writing) is still with us. She does not, as we had secretly hoped, live in Buffalo.

EXPLANATION REQUIRED: With George in a daze after talking with Harry, Uncle Billy introduces Ruth (offscreen) to some family friends. Here's what we are able to reconstruct of this exchange:

UNCLE BILLY
... bride to be. This is the new Mrs. Bailey. My nephew [inaudible] from Buffalo. These are all old friends of the Baileys.

RUTH BAILEY
Oh really?! Oh, what are their names? Let's see, now . . . Oh, of course, I've heard him speak of you. Oh!

UNCLE BILLY
Sure. . . . Just got in here now. We're taking her home, and I want to tell you that we're gonna give the biggest party this town ever saw.

RUTH BAILEY
Oh! Oh, that sounds wonderful!

Ruth's dialogue appears to have been dubbed—Patton is eating popcorn when she is supposed to be delivering this last line.

RANDOM THOUGHTS: Note that Harry's bride is wearing white gloves as she daintily munches on her popcorn while talking with George. *(0:37:21)* Our crack research reveals that proper glove etiquette calls for their removal before handling food. So don't let those clothes fool you—Ruth has an uncouth side as well!

CLOSER LOOK: OK, so it's no secret that this scene features George, Harry, Ruth, and Uncle Billy. But what you almost surely don't know is that there's another familiar character lurking in this scene. As George approaches Ruth to quiz her on Harry's job offer, we get an ever-so-brief glimpse of a mugging Ernie. *(37.16)* A split second later Harry walks past George in the foreground and hands Ernie (offscreen) the newlyweds' luggage. Ernie then carries the luggage out to the parking lot (visible in background). If Ernie is here to pick up Harry and Ruth, we're stumped as to why—that's what George and Uncle Billy came to do.

Harry's "Welcome Home" Party *(0:37:45)*

CLOSER LOOK: This scene opens with the Bailey family and other guests posing for a photograph on Mrs. Bailey's front porch. The photographer is George's cousin, Eustace Bailey. Look for him skirting past everyone, camera in hand, just after the picture is taken. *(0:37:57)* Photography must be Cousin Eustace's thing—he can also be seen taking photos at George and Mary's wedding send-off.

FILM ANECDOTES: Legend has it that the offscreen sound of Uncle Billy crashing into what sound like garbage cans was unscripted. As the story goes, a stage hand inadvertently knocked over some props at the end of the shot, prompting Thomas Mitchell to ad-lib, "I'm all right. I'm allllllllll right!" Unfortunately, the facts do not bear the story out. The script as it stood just prior to filming already called for Uncle Billy to crash into garbage cans. Now, the preproduction script *did not* include the "I'm all right" line, so we suppose that if the alleged mishap did occur it could have inspired Thomas Mitchell to improvise that line. But whatever the case, the scene was almost certainly reshot with proper sound effects.

RANDOM THOUGHTS: In case you haven't yet figured out that George isn't busting out of Bedford Falls anytime soon, the sound of a train whistle as George steps outside for a smoke serves as a not-so-subtle reminder that the train has once again "left the station" without him.

CLOSER LOOK: After hearing the train whistle, a sullen George pulls out the same three travel brochures that he was perusing earlier at the station. For one of the brochures all we can read is the heading "Europe." However, we are afforded a nice close-up of the other two. *(0:39:16)*

The brochure on the left reads: "South America/New York to Brazil–Uruguay–Argentina/Schedule and Passenger Rates." This particular brochure was distributed by the Munson Steamship Lines, which was an actual line based in New York City. (When George pulls out the same brochure at the train station *(0:35:29)*, the name *Munson* appears at the bottom.) The brochure on the right reads: "Travel with the Foremost Student Tours/College Travel Club." This was an actual travel club that operated during the 1930s.

MUSIC NOTES: As George and his mother share a moment on the front walkway, party guests dance inside the house to a wonderfully wistful tune called "Avalon." The song, which is about the romantic harbor town of Avalon on California's Catalina Island, was among the top hits of 1920 and a favorite of Benny Goodman's through the years. It was written by Al Jolson and Vincent Rose, though the two lost a lawsuit alleging that they lifted the melody from the Italian opera *Tosca*. The song appears in equally unheralded fashion in another American film classic, *Casablanca*. At the time Ilsa asks Sam to "play it," meaning "As Time Goes By," Sam is playing "Avalon."

George and Violet Downtown *(0:41:08)*

FILM ANECDOTES: It's impossible to figure this out from watching the film, but the final script reveals that Violet is closing up her beauty shop for the evening when she spies George across the street. Her shop is located in the space where the American Florist flower shop used to be, though it seems that the set designers didn't bother changing the storefront design for the shot as several floral arrangements appear in the shop's windows. Look for the key to the shop in Violet's right hand as she turns around and sees George. *(0:41:18)* The script confirms that the two men around her are salesmen who make regular sales calls on the beauty shop and are now angling for a date. A bizarre early version of this scene had George exchanging blows with one of them after the guy refused to stop hounding Violet.

CAST ANECDOTES: For the role of Violet, Capra was looking for what he described as a "good bad girl," and he sure found it in Gloria Grahame. This film was Grahame's first big break in Hollywood, where her sultry features made her a natural in the role of the temptress. Grahame went on to star in a number of solid films, including *Crossfire* (1947, Academy Award nomination for Best Supporting Actress), *In a Lonely Place* (1950, cast opposite Humphrey Bogart), *The Bad and the Beautiful* (1952, Academy Award for Best Supporting Actress), and *The Big Heat* (1953).

Though her film career was a success, her personal life was a bit of a mess. For one, she had serious hang-ups with her facial features, so much so that she had several cosmetic surgeries in an attempt to "fix" the appearance of her lips. The surgeries left her upper lip paralyzed, which only served to further fuel her insecurities.

Moreover, her love life was truly the stuff of movies. In the wake of one failed marriage, she married director Nicholas Ray in 1948. He was reputed to have a rather abusive personality, and they had a major falling out during the filming of *In a Lonely Place*, for which Ray was the director. Shortly thereafter Ray stumbled upon Grahame in, shall we say, close quarters with Ray's teenage stepson. Complicating matters even further, several years later Grahame married the kid (then in his early twenties) and had two children with him. Needless to say, the effect of this scandal on Grahame's career was not altogether positive.

5

GEORGE CALLS ON MARY

❝ He says it's the chance of a lifetime. ❞
—MARY HATCH

After his rather humiliating run-in with Violet, a brooding George soon finds himself in front of Mary's house, not entirely sure of his intentions. Mary, having been tipped off by Mrs. Bailey that George may come a-calling, is not about to let this golden opportunity slip through her hands. Donning a fetching party dress, Mary deftly exploits their dalliance on the night of the graduation dance by playing "Buffalo Gals" on the phonograph and presenting George with a caricature of him "lassoing" the moon. But her thoughtfulness appears to be lost on George, who mopes about and is, generally speaking, a complete pill. The visit quickly unravels on account of George's surly demeanor and George heads out the door in a huff.

Just seconds later a crestfallen Mary receives a phone call from George's old pal Sam Wainwright, who has been courting Mary from New York City. Mary sees that George has returned to fetch his hat and begins speaking flirtatiously with Sam in the hopes of making George jealous. Her scheme works and a curious George dawdles just long enough that he is within earshot when Sam asks Mary to put him on the phone. Sam, oblivious to the heat being generated at the Hatch household, jokingly accuses George of trying to steal his girl—an accusation that George vehemently denies.

As Sam gives them both the lowdown on his new business venture, George and Mary realize that they are cheek to cheek on the phone. Their physical proximity is too much for either of them to bear, and George soon finds himself blurting out a heartfelt, if unconventional, profession of his love. Mrs. Hatch, who has done her level best all evening to prevent these two from hooking up, will have to get used to George, because by the end of the night there's not much doubt that these two are gonna get hitched.

George Calls on Mary *(0:42:28)*

CLOSER LOOK: The mailbox outside Mary's house reads, "Mrs. J. W. Hatch." Curiously, we're never told the whereabouts or fate of Mr. Hatch. *(0:42:36)* However, given that he's not mentioned on the mailbox, and that he's a no-show at his own daughter's wedding, we can safely assume that, wherever he is, he's not coming back! Another unanswered question regarding the Hatch family is whether Mary has any other siblings besides Marty. Is there any chance at all that Mary has a younger sister? One can only dream.

MUSIC NOTES: We've heard snippets of "Buffalo Gals" before now, but this scene offers a longer listen. "Buffalo Gals" is an old minstrel song that was composed back in 1844 by Cool White (aka John Hodges), who performed in a minstrel group called the Virginia Serenaders. Variations of the song have arisen through the years, such as "Lubly Fan" and "Dance with a Dolly." Performers also frequently swapped out "Buffalo" for the name of the town where the song was being performed (e.g., "Boston Gals," "Richmond Gals"). Ironically, while the song seems innocent enough, it's actually about Buffalo, New York, prostitutes being courted by gents in the rough-and-tumble days that came with the completion of the Erie Canal.

The following lyrics can be heard on the record that Mary plays for George—feel free to sing along:

As I was lumb'rin down the street
Down the street, down the street,
A handsome gal I chanced to meet
Oh! She was fair to view

I asked her if she'd have some fun
Have some fun, have some fun
Her feet covered up the whole sidewalk
As she stood close by me

Buffalo gals, can't you come out tonight
Can't you come out tonight, can't you come out tonight
Buffalo gals, can't you come out tonight
And dance by the light of the moon

The second verse is an oddity, as it typically goes, *I asked her if she'd have a talk/Have a talk, have a talk/Her feet took up the whole sidewalk/And left no room for me.* For your amusement we have included three other verses, none of which are used in the film:

> *I asked her if she'd have a dance*
> *Have a dance, have a dance*
> *I thought that I might have a chance*
> *To shake a foot with her*

> *I danced with a gal with a hole in her stockin'*
> *And her hip kept a rockin' and her toe kept a-knockin'*
> *I danced with a gal with a hole in her stockin'*
> *And we danced by the light of the moon*

> *O yes, pretty boys, we're a comin' out tonight*
> *We're comin' out tonight, we're comin' out tonight*
> *O yes, pretty boys, were comin' out tonight*
> *To dance by the light of the moon*

CLOSER LOOK: Use freeze-frame to read the record label for "Buffalo Gals" as it plays on the old Victrola phonograph. The label attributes the song to "Arthur Black and His Orchestra" and shows Velvet Tone as the recording label. Velvet Tone was an actual "budget" label produced by Columbia Records from the late 1920s to the early 1930s. But the discography for Velvet Tone does not include any recordings by a band named Arthur Black and His Orchestra, or of "Buffalo Gals," by anyone. Nor is the design of the label itself consistent with that of actual Velvet Tone labels.

So what's the story here? Well it appears that we are all victims of an inside joke. The film's assistant director, you see, was one Arthur Black.

EXPLANATION REQUIRED: When Mrs. Hatch asks Mary what George wants, Mary declares, "He's making violent love to me, mother!" If you blush every time you hear this line, blush no more. In the old days "making love" basically meant "courting" or "flirting," not "going all the way." So relax. Your wholesome perception of Mary can remain intact.

CLOSER LOOK: It's clear from this scene that Mrs. Hatch is not a big fan of George—and the feeling is apparently mutual. Check out the scowls the two of them exchange as George grabs the phone. In fact, Mrs. Hatch is so distraught over George's presence that she calls her own daughter an "idiot" for putting George on the phone. We're not entirely sure why Mrs. Hatch is down on George, but we have a pretty good idea that it's about money: Sam has it, and George doesn't.

JUST WONDERING: What in the world was Sam thinking when he placed this phone call to Mary? Sam has been courting Mary for some time, yet he phones her from his swanky office in New York City with a mink-shawl-wearing floozy draped all over him! Huh?! Sam's business skills may not be in doubt, but his social skills sure are.

CLOSER LOOK: Look for the lighted sign outside Sam's office window that reads "Hotel Piccadilly." *(0:47:39)* This was an actual hotel in New York City back in the 1930s, located at 227 West 45th Street. The hotel's address tells us that Sam's office is located in tony Times Square. Also visible from Sam's office window is a sign for Chevrolet; directly beneath it scrolls an ad that reads "Genuine Fisher No Draft Ventilation."

The name *Fisher* refers to the Fisher Body Company, which became a division of General Motors in 1926. The term *no draft ventilation* refers to a feature introduced on all GM cars in 1933, which consisted of triangular side windows that pivoted to create controlled cabin air flow. This technology was no substitute for air conditioning (which was not introduced in automobiles until 1939), but was no doubt better than just rolling down the windows.

Unfortunately, while GM first introduced "no draft ventilation" in January 1933, this scene is set in June 1932. So unless this is an advertisement for next year's models, we have stumbled across a most obscure film gaffe.

EXPLANATION REQUIRED: When the film shows George and Mary on the phone listening to Sam explain that he wants to make plastics from soybeans, listen for the voice of Sam's business partner on the phone as he jokingly corrects Sam that he means "chili beans," not soybeans.

DID YOU KNOW? Is Sam really going to get rich making plastics from soybeans? At first blush it may sound like a crackpot idea, but actually the concept is scientifically sound. Indeed, the likely inspiration for this plotline was Henry Ford, who in the early 1930s developed a strange affinity for the humble soybean. Ford devoted considerable financial resources toward developing various uses for the commodity, including soy-based plastics. Eventually Ford incorporated various parts made of soybean meal into his automobiles, and even developed a prototype plastic car body molded from soybeans.

Thus, it is historically plausible not only that George would have read about soybean-based plastics before 1932 (the year of Sam's phone call), but also that Sam would have made headway with the idea, although the technology was certainly not advanced enough to make a clear plastic suitable for airplane hoods.

RANDOM THOUGHTS: Sam boasts that the idea of making plastics from soybeans is the best thing since "radio." Radio was invented at the turn of the century. Here are a few things invented between then and the early 1930s (the time of Sam's remark)—you be the judge on how Sam's invention stacks up: the airplane, color photography, instant coffee, the bra, stainless steel, air conditioning, liquid-fueled rockets, television, penicillin, the jet engine, and, of course, sliced bread.

FILM ANECDOTES: More film lore surrounds George and Mary's torrid exchange while on the phone. As the story goes, this being Stewart's first film since returning from the war, he was feeling a bit off his romancing game—so much so that he kept delaying filming of the scene. But the first take was so electric that Capra gave the order to "print it" despite the fact that the actors had omitted several lines of dialogue.

While it may have happened that way, we suspect otherwise. First, it turns out that no dialogue was dropped. The dialogue in the scene, as shot, is nearly identical to the dialogue in the script as it stood prior to filming. Second, given Capra's reputation for shooting multiple takes, it's unlikely that Capra could have resisted filming a few more takes as insurance. Consistent with our theory, the production materials show that more than a week's worth of filming went into capturing the scenes at the Hatch house.

Note that Stewart fails to lay a kiss of any length on Reed. That's because in 1930 the film industry began self-regulating (read: censoring) film content by means of an absurdly restrictive set of guidelines known as the Motion Picture Production Code. Among other things, the code prohibited "excessive and lustful kissing," which in practice apparently translated into no kiss being allowed to last more than three seconds or so.

RANDOM THOUGHTS: Before moving on, let's review George's actions during the last few hours. First he tells his mother that he's going to find a girl to "do some passionate necking with." Then he finds himself standing on a street corner in downtown Bedford Falls ogling girls as they pass by. *(0:41:14)* Then he tries to pick up Violet and take her to "the Falls," surely Bedford Falls' version of Lover's Lane. Then, just minutes later, we find him over at Mary's house professing his love for her. Now that is some turn of events!

6

GEORGE AND MARY'S WEDDING DAY

❝ Welcome home, Mr. Bailey. ❞
—MARY BAILEY

Brace yourself for yet another whirlwind day in George's life. After we get stiffed on an invitation to the wedding ceremony, we pick up with George and Mary leaving their reception. Bound for a fabulous two-week honeymoon vacation, it looks as if George is finally going to bust out of Bedford Falls. But everything comes to a screeching halt on the ride to the train station when Ernie spots a crowd gathering in front of the bank and quickly deduces that a bank run is in progress.

Over Mary's protestations George heads back to the Building & Loan, where he is greeted by a throng of panicked shareholders. He tries to reason with them, but they're having none of it. They want their money and they want it now. Complicating matters is the fact that Potter, ever the opportunist, is scheming to put the Building & Loan out of business by offering to buy out its shareholders at a steep discount. When the shareholders get wind of Potter's offer and start heading out the door, Mary saves the day by offering up their honeymoon kitty to pay the shareholders off. This enables the Building & Loan to close its doors for the day still solvent, albeit by the slimmest of margins.

Thankfully, not even a bank run can ruin George and Mary's wedding day. As George is busy placating the shareholders, Mary slips out the door, and with a little help from Bert and Ernie, creates a makeshift bridal suite for their wedding night. Somehow Mary has managed to acquire the old Granville house, which, despite its ramshackle condition, provides a thoroughly romantic setting for their first night together as husband and wife.

The Wedding Send-Off *(0:50:13)*

DID YOU KNOW?: George does not wear a wedding band during the film. Double ring ceremonies were not in vogue in America until World War II, when this largely European tradition caught on with American servicemen.

CLOSER LOOK: The list of attendees at George and Mary's wedding reception is a strange one indeed. No Uncle Billy (we're told later that he was trying to hold down the fort at the bank). No Harry Bailey. No Marty Hatch. No Sam Wainwright. And of all of George's friends around town, only Mr. Gower gets the nod. (Ernie is there for the send-off, but if his taxi driver's uniform is any indication, he's strictly hired help.)

As for those who are in attendance, how did Violet make the cut? Mary never liked Violet and thought all along that she was trying to steal George away from her. Indeed, her suspicions were well founded as George was just one climb up Mt. Bedford away from taking his relationship with Violet to another level. Still, in a small town like Bedford Falls, a friend is a friend, and George sees to it that Violet gets an invite.

CLOSER LOOK: Did you notice who catches Mary's bouquet? It's her good friend, Violet! *(0:50:17)* Unfortunately, Violet never enjoys the benefits that are supposed to befall one who catches a bride's bouquet. Some twelve years later Violet still had not married.

DID YOU KNOW? George wasn't kidding when he tells Ernie that he and Mary are planning to "shoot the works" on their honeymoon. George and Mary set out on their trip with $2,000 in cash. In 2006 dollars, George and Mary's kitty is worth around $29,500. Now that would have been some trip.

RANDOM THOUGHTS: Ernie passes along a bottle of champagne to George and Mary, compliments of Bert. It's certainly a nice gesture on Bert's part, but hold on a second here. This is June 1932, which means that Prohibition is still in effect. So what in the world is Bert doing gifting alcohol during Prohibition? Quick! Somebody call the police! Oh yeah, that would be Bert.

HISTORY LESSON: With the ratification of the 18th Amendment to the United States Constitution, it was illegal from January 16, 1920, to December 5, 1933, to manufacture or sell any drink containing more than .05 percent alcohol. Prohibition proponents, mostly descendants of early American settlers, believed that alcohol abuse among newer immigrants was tearing the moral fabric of American society. World War I then set the stage for

Prohibition when Americans in large part bought into the notion that abstinence from alcohol was a patriotic way to further the war effort.

Intended to decrease lawlessness, Prohibition had the opposite effect. Bars were replaced by an even greater number of illegal speakeasies, average Americans were forced to break the law just to have a recreational beer, and the newly created bootlegging industry served as the foundation for the kudzu-like growth of gangster activity in America. While Republicans held fast in their support of Prohibition throughout the Hoover administration, after Democrat Franklin Delano Roosevelt defeated Hoover in 1932, Prohibition's days were numbered.

The Bank Run *(0:51:47)*

CLOSER LOOK: Although we've seen the Building & Loan's offices once before back in 1919, this scene offers the first good look at the office layout. Take a look at the floor diagram that we've created for the location of various office details and events. Note that the interior design is surprisingly consistent with the building's exterior and even incorporates the building's flattened corner into the design of George's office. *(0:13:19)*

FILM ANECDOTES: The office mascot at the Building & Loan is a raven. The raven actually has a name—Jimmy the Raven. Listen for Jimmy Stewart muttering "Look out, Jimmy" as he hurdles the office counter during the

THE BAILEY BROTHERS BUILDING & LOAN ASSOCIATION

1. Location on Genesee Street of street-level entrance to Building & Loan.

2. Window from which Uncle Billy, Tilly, and Eustace yell to George after George picks up his suitcase.

3. Where George jumps the counter during the bank run.

4. Tilly and Eustace's shared desk.

5. Eustace's adding machine.

6. Tilly's phone operator equipment.

7. Location of Peter Bailey's portrait at the time of the bank run.

8. Location of the loving cup from the Charleston contest (resting on a file cabinet).

9. Where George pleads with shareholders not to sell their shares to Potter.

10. Where George talks on the phone with Harry on Christmas Eve.

11. Entrance to the conference room where George meets with the bank examiner.

12. Where Violet wipes lipstick off George's cheek and wishes him "Merry Christmas."

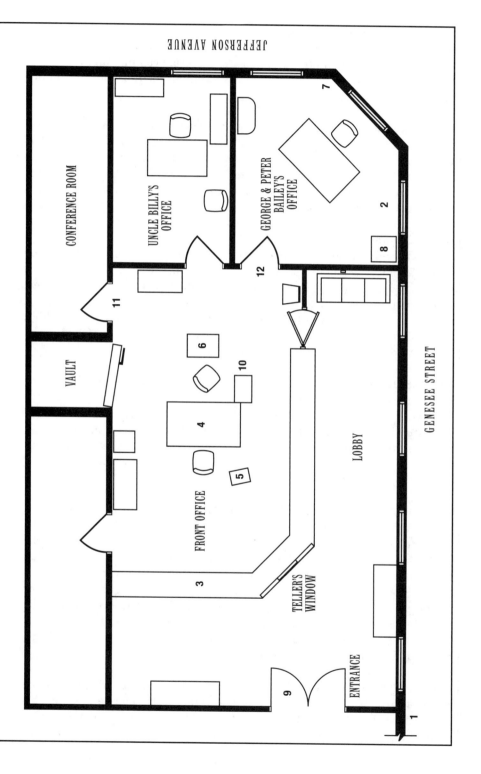

JEFFERSON AVENUE

CONFERENCE ROOM

UNCLE BILLY'S OFFICE

GEORGE & PETER BAILEY'S OFFICE

7

2

8

12

11

VAULT

6

10

4

5

FRONT OFFICE

3

LOBBY

TELLER'S WINDOW

ENTRANCE

9

1

GENESEE STREET

bank run. *(0:53:06)* Jimmy the Raven was a favorite of director Frank Capra and appeared in some of his other films, including *You Can't Take It with You*. Including Jimmy in the film was another great casting call by Capra as the bird contributes nicely to the quirky, family-owned feel of the Building & Loan.

HISTORY LESSON: As George walks back to his office, a newspaper sits on Tilly's desk with the headline SENATE DEFEATS BONUS. *(0:53:12)* This headline refers to a most bizarre and unfortunate event in American history. For more than a decade, American veterans of World War I lobbied vociferously for additional monetary compensation for their military service. In May 1932, tens of thousands of Depression-battered veterans made camp on the outskirts of Washington, D.C., and formed protests demanding passage of a long-pursued "veteran's bonus" bill.

The bill made it through the House of Representatives, but on June 17, 1932, the Senate voted it down. Incensed, the so-called Bonus Army refused to leave the city. This prompted President Hoover to call in the real army, which proceeded to use guns, bayonets, army tanks, and even the cavalry to remove its own war veterans from the nation's capital. Incredibly, three of America's most celebrated war heroes—MacArthur, Eisenhower, and Patton—orchestrated the veterans' military ouster.

FILM ANECDOTES: Capra's use of the SENATE DEFEATS BONUS headline likely stems from the fact that he himself was a veteran of World War I. We give Capra credit for using another reality-based headline, but unfortunately the timing of the event does not quite coincide with the setting for the scene. The Senate's vote on the bonus bill took place in June 1932, whereas the bank run scene is set (according to the film's production materials) in October 1932.

CLOSER LOOK: If you're wondering where Potter learned his dictatorial ways, look no further than the bust of Napoleon in Potter's office. *(53:53)* Thankfully, while Napoleon had his sights set on conquering the world, Potter would settle for Bedford Falls. Potter should know, though, that Napoleon's run did not end so well. After the British finally got their hands on him, he spent the rest of his life imprisoned on a craggy island in the middle of the South Atlantic. Anyway, Napoleon's bust (there are actually two) can be seen several different times in Potter's office at the bank. The bust is one of several ornamental pieces that migrated from Potter's home office to his new digs after he took over the bank.

RANDOM THOUGHTS: Uncle Billy sort of implies that he missed the wedding because of the bank run. But George has seen this act before and thinks his scatterbrained uncle just plain forgot, telling him that he can take the string off his finger now. But let's give poor Uncle Billy the benefit of the doubt and say that if he did forget, it was only because he got tied up with the bank run debacle.

Anyway, what's weirder? Uncle Billy forgetting George and Mary's wedding, or the fact that no one from the wedding bothered to *track Uncle Billy down*? And don't forget that he missed the wedding *and* the reception. There are only so many places that a man can be in Bedford Falls, and a phone call to the most obvious one—the Building & Loan—would have solved the mystery. Whatever the case, Uncle Billy has got to come up with a better way to remember things—the strings just ain't working.

CLOSER LOOK: Two portraits hang in George's office. One is of his father, beneath which appears the following words of inspiration: "All you can take with you is that which you've given away." *(0:54:48)* The other is of America's thirty-first president, Herbert Hoover. Look for it by the window closest to the door. *(0:53:42)* Hoover was still in office in October 1932 when this scene was set, but not for long. By that time he was not exactly a popular guy, as millions of poverty-stricken Americans held him accountable for failing to pull the country out of its economic death spiral. And just one month later Franklin Delano Roosevelt scored a landslide victory over Hoover in the 1932 presidential election.

JUST WONDERING: Ever wonder whether George and Mary won the Charleston contest? Given their performance, you would think they would have been a shoo-in to take home the hardware. Well, the bank run sequence provides evidence that they were, in fact, victorious. In the scene where George and Uncle Billy confer in George's office, a loving cup–style trophy sits on a cabinet by the window closest to the door. Look for it as George stands at the window just before getting on the phone with Potter. *(0:53:42)* We compared this trophy to the one wielded by Harry at the dance *(0:21:23)*, and there's not much doubt that it's the same one.

HISTORY LESSON: The Bedford Falls bank run was a by-product of the Great Depression, the most severe and prolonged economic downturn America has ever endured. Beginning in 1929, banks were failing left and right as bad investments in the stock market and overly risky loans came home to roost. Nervous bank customers decided en masse that maybe their mattresses weren't such a bad place to store their money after all. But because banks were required to keep on hand only a fraction of deposited funds at any given time, they did not have enough cash to repay all their depositors at once. George's explanation of this concept to the shareholders falls on deaf ears.

Between 1929 and March 1933 some 9,000 banks went bust. Only after President Roosevelt took office in March 1933 did things start to turn around. Roosevelt's first order of business was to shut down the entire national banking system and declare a two-week "bank holiday."

Meanwhile, Roosevelt went to work, largely through a series of his legendary fireside chats, trying to convince a skittish public that the banking system was indeed trustworthy. Depositors slowly returned, and, with the institution of a federal deposit insurance system in the summer of 1933, the bank run problem was largely put to rest.

FILM ANECDOTES: Another storied tale from the film relates to the sequence where George doles out get-me-by funds to Building & Loan shareholders. As this one goes, Capra secretly instructed the actress playing Mrs. Davis, Ellen Corby, to request an even smaller amount ($17.50) than called for in the script, with the intention of surprising Jimmy Stewart. It worked, leading Stewart to plant an impromptu kiss on Corby. This is one story that actually can be confirmed, not only through the preproduction script (it called for Corby to ask for more than twice the amount and did not include the kiss from Stewart) but also through Corby's recollection. And if anyone ought to know, it's she!

RANDOM THOUGHTS: Is there any way to figure out George and Mary's wedding date? Well, sort of. We know from the film's production materials that the wedding is set in October 1932. As for the wedding date, the Building & Loan's office clock provides a clue. As the Building & Loan crew counts down the last few seconds to closing, the film cuts to a shot of the clock. *(0:58:41)* Note that the clock has a third hand for the date, which is set on the 30th day of the month. Hence, their wedding date is October 30, 1932, right?

Well, we thought so anyway, until we discovered that in 1932, the 30th day of October actually landed on a Sunday. What's wrong with that, you ask? Would you expect a small-town bank in the 1930s to be open on Sunday? So if we conclude that their wedding day is Sunday, October 30, 1932, we must tally another film gaffe for nonsensical banking hours. On the other hand, if we conclude that the clock's calendar setting is wrong, then we are stumped on the date.

By the way, if you're thinking that the wedding must have been on a Saturday, consider that the bank is supposed to be open at 2:45 P.M. when the bank run begins to unfold *(0:53:35)*—not what you would expect from a bank on a Saturday. Indeed, the signage on the bank's front door (albeit some thirteen years later) shows 1 P.M. as the closing time on Saturdays *(1:20:52)*

RANDOM THOUGHTS: It appears that the characters in *It's a Wonderful Life* were typical Americans when it came to skirting the law during Prohibition. First Harry plans to drink gin on graduation night. Then Bert the cop gives George and Mary a bottle of champagne on their wedding day. And now in this scene, George, Uncle Billy, Eustace, and Tilly break out a bottle of bootlegged firewater to celebrate the Building & Loan surviving the bank run.

MUSIC NOTES: While celebrating their having saved the Building & Loan, George, Uncle Billy, Eustace, and Tilly parade around the office humming "Stars and Stripes Forever" by John Philip Sousa.

The Bridal Suite *(1:00:07)*

JUST WONDERING: Just how and when did Mary come to acquire the old Granville house? It could be that she secretly bought the house before the wedding with the intention of surprising George when they returned from their honeymoon. But an earlier script had her buying the house *during* the bank run. If that was the case, here's how things might have transpired. As George pays off shareholders, Mary slips out, heads for town hall, and purchases the abandoned house by paying the back taxes with her own savings and, perhaps, a cash refund from their honeymoon train tickets. She then enlists the help of Bert and Ernie and bedecks the house with makeshift wedding night accoutrements. All of this would have to have taken place in just over three hours, as the bank run starts around 2:45 P.M. (according to a clock in the office) and ends at 6:00 P.M. (when the Building & Loan closes).

CLOSER LOOK: Bert, Ernie, and a handyman hang several posters around the house in an effort to create a little ambience. One poster appearing at the bottom of the stairs (by the entrance to their makeshift bedroom) shows a child in a nightgown holding an old candle lamp. *(1:01:36)* On the child's shoulder is, of all things, a car tire, and beneath the child a slogan reads, "Time to Retire—Get a Fisk." This clever product slogan was part of a popular advertising campaign launched by the Fisk Rubber Company, which back in 1928 was a major American car tire manufacturer. Fisk was bought out in the late 1930s by the company that eventually became Uniroyal.

Three more posters hang in the "dining room." Two of them read "Winter in Florida—Gulf Tours" and "No Other Vacations Like These in U.S.A." The third one shows an ocean liner and reads "Cruise the South Seas—Luxurious Travel on the Dollar Line." *(1:02:08)* The Dollar Line was a popular cruise ship line that serviced the South Seas out of San Francisco from 1924 to 1938. Unable to weather the economic "perfect storm" known as the Great Depression, the line was eventually taken over by the U.S. government and renamed the American President Lines. Most of the liners were lost during World War II after being commandeered by the government for the war effort.

CLOSER LOOK: In the bedroom of the honeymoon suite (which ends up being the dining room once the house gets fixed up), Mary has carefully laid out her nightgown and a pair of pajamas for George. *(1:01:39)* We say, forget the nightgown, Mary looks stunning even in the kitchen apron that she's wearing. In the dining room (which becomes the living room post rehab), Mary is roasting chickens in the fireplace. To power the spit, Mary ingeniously connects it to a hand-crank phonograph, using a large spool as an interface. For dessert, they're having wedding cake, of course, which serves as the centerpiece on the dining room table. Check out the bride and groom figurines on the cake. *(1:02:12)*

CLOSER LOOK: Above the fireplace a framed piece of what looks like needlework reads "The Lord Will Provide." *(1:02:43)*

MUSIC NOTES: To set a romantic mood, Mary plays a dreamy, hypnotic Hawaiian tune called "Song of the Islands." The song was written by Charles E. King, a popular Hawaiian music composer in his day. Originally written in 1915, the song experienced a revival of sorts in 1929 when it was used in a film called *Melody Lane.* (Don't bother trying to rent this film as there is no known surviving copy.) The song also appeared in two films in 1942, one of which was a musical by the same name starring Betty Grable and the seemingly ubiquitous Thomas Mitchell (Uncle Billy). The first part of the verse heard in *It's a Wonderful Life* is a little tough to make out, so here's some help: *Islands of Hawaii / Where skies of blue are calling me / Where balmy airs and golden moonlight . . .*

MUSIC NOTES: The "bridal suite" scene ends with Bert and Ernie putting on a little vaudeville routine, serenading the newlyweds with a fine rendition of "I Love You Truly." Bert and Ernie go off script a bit here when they sing *Life with its shadows, life with its tears.* It's supposed to be *Life with its sorrow, life with its tear.*

JUST WONDERING: When Mary whispers to George what she had wished for years ago when they threw rocks at the Granville house, do you think George hears a word of it? It's the same ear that George lost his hearing in during the sledding mishap.

RANDOM THOUGHTS: However charming this night was, the rest of the honeymoon surely had to be a letdown. According to George, they were going to stay in the "highest hotels," drink the "oldest champagne," eat the "richest caviar," and hear the "hottest music." Instead, they will stay on the ground floor of an abandoned house, drink Bert the cop's bootlegged sparkling wine, eat spaghetti dinners at Martini's, and hear yesterday's hits on Martini's juke box.

CAST ANECDOTES: The romantic lives of Jimmy Stewart and Donna Reed bore little resemblance to those of George and Mary Bailey. Stewart was the consummate Hollywood bachelor, romantically linked through the years to quite a few leading ladies, including Margaret Sullavan, Ginger Rogers, Marlene Dietrich, and Olivia de Havilland. He managed to remain single until 1949, when at the age of forty-one he exchanged vows with Gloria McLean, who was ten years his junior.

Reed went to the altar three times, the first time at the tender age of twenty-one. In 1942, just as she was making a name for herself, and with a myriad of suitors vying for her attention, Reed inexplicably married her regular makeup artist, a curiously unassuming man named Bill Tuttle. The marriage ended as mysteriously and quietly as it began, with Reed traveling to Juarez, Mexico, in 1945 to obtain a "quickie" divorce.

On the way back from Mexico she got bumped from her flight. This seeming bit of bad luck soon proved otherwise when her scheduled flight crashed while trying to land at the Burbank, California, airport, killing all twenty-four aboard.

Just a few months later, Reed remarried, this time to her agent and confidant, Tony Owens, who seemed to have had romantic aspirations for Reed since they first met. After a rather tempestuous eighteen-year marriage, they called it quits in 1971. Finally, in 1974 Reed married a retired army colonel named Grover Asmus who, once smitten, launched a full-scale campaign for her hand until she finally surrendered.

7

MOVING DAY FOR THE MARTINIS

" You wouldn't mind living in the nicest house in
town, buying your wife a lot of fine clothes, a
couple of business trips to New York a year,
maybe once in a while Europe? You wouldn't
mind that, would you, George? **"**

—HENRY F. POTTER

The Building & Loan's goal through the years has been to make home-
ownership a reality for Bedford Fallsians of modest means. And there
is perhaps no better example of the Building & Loan's achievements on that
front than the Martini family. For years the Martinis had no choice but to
rent from Bedford Falls' resident slumlord, Henry F. Potter. But on this
momentous day in June 1934, we find the Martinis finally moving into a
home of their own, located in a bucolic development known as Bailey Park.
Thanks to that "measly one-horse institution," no more will the Martinis
have to "live like pigs" in Potter's Field.

Reflecting their commitment to the Building & Loan's shareholders,
George and Mary gladly pitch in to help the Martinis move across town. As
George and Mary oversee the christening ceremony for the Martinis' new
home, the entrepreneurial Sam Wainwright stops by for an impromptu visit.
Though Sam is a childhood friend, George is unnerved by his presence,
undoubtedly because Sam serves as a walking reminder of how George
never made it out of Bedford Falls.

Meanwhile, across town, Potter is hatching yet another plan to sink
the Building & Loan. Potter's rent collector has advised him that the Bailey

Park development is cutting into his real estate profits. So Potter decides to offer George a job, knowing full well that the Building & Loan's days would be numbered without George at the helm. Potter dangles an impressive employment package: a salary that is nearly 900 percent higher than George's current draw, and the prospect of regular business junkets to New York and beyond. This all sounds swell to George, until he gets a bad vibe from a handshake with the old codger and, in an instant, wises up to Potter's deceitful plan.

George returns home late that night feeling as glum as ever about the purgatory he knows as Bedford Falls. As rough as this day has been, George needs some good news, and lo and behold Mary has some: George, it seems, has "lassoed a stork." Mary is pregnant!

Moving Day for the Martinis *(1:03:46)*

CLOSER LOOK: Can you spot the various animals that make cameos as the Martinis pack up their belongings and head for Bailey Park? Some are more obvious than others. First, there is the Martinis' goat, which bums a ride with George and Mary. Check out a concerned Donna Reed taking firm hold of the goat's horns after realizing that they pose a serious health threat to the little girls in the back seat! *(1:04:26)*

Two other animals also get a lift from the Baileys. Keep your eye on the third Martini daughter as she climbs into the backseat—she has two puppies tucked under her arms. *(1:04:20)* Also appearing in the scene is a dog, some rabbits (in a cage on Mr. Martini's truck), and a rather sad-looking turkey, which can be found in the box that George carries out of the Martinis' house. *(1:03:52)*

RANDOM THOUGHTS: We've always thought that Bailey Park was an outstanding name for a baseball stadium. And the same would go for Potter's Field, were it not for the fact that the term *potter's field* means a field that is used for burying the bodies of indigent and unidentified persons. That being the case, Potter might just as well have named his development Potter's Cemetery!

JUST WONDERING: The Martinis seem like a great family, but how are their pets—particularly the goat—going to go over in the suburban environs of Bailey Park?

FILM ANECDOTES: If the scraggly hills of Bailey Park do not exactly remind you of rural New York State, it's because the scene was filmed in the foothills outside Los Angeles.

HISTORY LESSON: The fact that the Martinis can afford a new house is particularly impressive given that by 1934 America was deep into the throes of the Great Depression. While many folks believe that the stock market crash of October 1929 was the cause of the Great Depression, in truth it was simply the first tangible symptom of an already sick economy. Throughout the 1920s, economic instability in America grew undetected as industrial and agricultural production far outpaced consumer consumption. Complicating matters was the fact that the European economy was still struggling mightily to right itself in the aftermath of World War I. The economic house of cards eventually collapsed with the 1929 stock market crash.

After that, things really got ugly. From 1929 to 1933 the unemployment rate rose from around 3 percent to a staggering 25 percent, which translates to more than 13 million people unable to find work. And those numbers don't account for the millions more who were forced to take pay cuts and reduced hours. At one point, home foreclosures were averaging 1,000 per day. After taking office in 1933, President Roosevelt tried every trick in the book to jump-start the economy, but nothing seemed to work. In 1939, more than a decade after the crash, unemployment was still in excess of 17 percent.

DID YOU KNOW? George and Mary's blessing for the Martinis goes like this:

Bread! That this house may never know hunger.
Salt! That life may always have flavor.
And wine! That joy and prosperity may reign forever.

This blessing is something of a cross between a Polish wedding tradition of presenting newlyweds with bread, salt, and wine, and a Russian house-warming tradition of bringing bread and salt to new home owners.

FILM ANECDOTES: Look for the Martinis making the sign of the cross during the christening ceremony. *(1:05:11)* RKO's in-house lawyers advised director Frank Capra to omit this religious reference on the grounds that British censors were doing the same. Other stuff flagged by the legal wonks as unacceptable under the stifling provisions of the Motion Picture Production Code included: "My answer is nuts to you!"; "I hate this dang place"; "I wish to God I'd never been born"; "pulling the chain"; "impotent"; "jerk"; and "lousy." Lest there be any doubt about the code's impact, none of this made it into the film.

RANDOM THOUGHTS: It's probably a good thing that Sam and his wife have a chauffeur and limousine as they have some 1,000 miles to cover on their trip to Florida. Next time how about bucking up for a couple of first-class train tickets?

CLOSER LOOK: The automobiles owned by George and Sam pretty much sum up their respective financial well-being. In contrast to George's clunker of a Dodge touring car, the well-to-do Sam shows up at the Martini house in one of the finest automobiles of its time, a Duesenberg town car. *(1:04:58)* Founded by two German brothers, Duesenberg Motors opened up shop in Indianapolis in 1920. Just a year later, they took the racing world by storm by building the first American-made racecar to win the International Grand Prix at Le Mans. Duesenberg cars went on to win the Indianapolis 500 in 1924, 1925, and 1927.

The company's stated goal was to make the finest luxury automobiles in the world, and, with the car that appears in *It's a Wonderful Life,* they pretty much succeeded. This particular car was manufactured around 1930 and retailed for some $16,000 (that's $213,000 in 2006 dollars). It was first owned by actress Dolores Del Rio before being acquired by a company that specialized in renting cars to movie studios, hence its appearance in *It's a Wonderful Life.* Today, were the car not resting comfortably in a private collection, it would surely fetch seven figures at auction. The Murphy-style town car body was one of only a handful ever made and, as you can see in the film, it featured an open-air driver's cabin with an enclosed passenger cabin. While the open-air design may not have been very practical for, say, Sam's 1,000-mile road trip to Florida, it made for an unmistakable show of status.

CAST ANECDOTES: The actor playing Sam Wainwright, Frank Albertson, plays a far less likable millionaire in another film classic, *Psycho* (1960). His oilman character gets his money stolen by eventual Bates Motel guest/victim Marion Crane.

CLOSER LOOK: George seems to have developed a genuine disdain for his poor little car, perhaps because it's a constant reminder of his modest lifestyle. After Sam pulls away, a frustrated George gives the driver's-side door a mean-spirited kick. The door does get its revenge later in the film, though. After George meets with Potter on Christmas Eve, the door will not open, forcing George to climb into the driver's seat. *(1:35:20)* Then, an hour or so later, George crashes into a tree, and the door inexplicably refuses to close. *(1:37:41)*

Potter Summons George to a Meeting *(1:07:31)*

EXPLANATION REQUIRED: The film offers no explanation of how George gets word way out in Bailey Park that Potter wants to see him. That's because the segue between the two scenes got cut. Before filming, the script called for quirky Cousin Eustace to ride up on his bicycle, just after Sam drove off, with urgent news that Potter wanted to meet with George. George was to then have trouble starting his car, prompting Eustace to jokingly offer up his bicycle.

CLOSER LOOK: Potter's desk is covered with creepy antiques. Among them is a cigarette lighter, a globe-shaped lamp with a dragon motif, a set for making wax seals, an ornate decanter set, an Asian ink well, and a rather ominous-looking metal casting of a human skull.

FILM ANECDOTES: Potter refers to Building & Loan shareholders as a bunch of "garlic eaters," a thinly veiled, disparaging reference to their Italian heritage. While RKO's legal department flagged this term as offensive dialogue, the film's director, Frank Capra, being a first-generation Italian immigrant himself, saw fit to keep it in.

DID YOU KNOW?: By the time he made *It's a Wonderful Life*, Capra was a major force in Hollywood, having already racked up five Academy Award nominations for Best Picture and five more for Best Director. Of these he won for Best Director three times (*It Happened One Night*, *Mr. Deeds Goes to Town*, and *You Can't Take It with You*) and for Best Picture once (*You Can't Take It with You*). His films from the 1930s—and specifically the revenue generated by those films—were responsible for elevating Columbia Pictures from a B-movie house to a major film studio. By 1938, Capra's popularity had reached such heights that he graced the cover of *Time* magazine.

It's a Wonderful Life actually marked the beginning of the decline of Capra's directing career. It was his first picture after a four-year hiatus from directing feature films brought about by World War II. Though he succeeded in recapturing the Capra magic of years past, the film felt more like a failure when it underachieved both at the box office and the Academy Awards. After *It's a Wonderful Life*, Capra directed a series of uninspired films and seemed to lose track of the formula that had made his earlier films so enduring. Indeed, even a remake of one of his own pictures—*Pocketful of Miracles* remaking *Lady for a Day*—missed the mark. His many successes notwithstanding, Capra gained a reputation for developing hokey story lines, which ultimately led film critics to call his work "Capra-corn."

JUST WONDERING: Just what does the F stand for in Henry F. Potter? We are never told, but perhaps it's short for *fer-de-lance*. (Look it up.)

RANDOM THOUGHTS: George tells Potter that he's making $45 per week, which equals $2,340 annually. $2,340 in 1934 has the consumer purchasing power in 2006 of about $35,350. In contrast, the $20,000 annual salary that Potter offers George is equivalent to a whopping $302,000 in 2006. Throw in a couple of business trips to New York and Europe, and who could blame George for thinking, however briefly, that his ship really had come in?

CLOSER LOOK: Look for the portrait of Potter (or perhaps it's one of his ancestors) on the wall by the office door. *(1:07:53)* A similar portrait appears in two other places during the film: Potter's study, when Potter talks on the telephone with George during the bank run *(0:53:53)*, and the lobby of the Bedford Falls Trust & Savings Bank, when Uncle Billy loses the deposit *(1:20:18)*.

RANDOM THOUGHTS: This sequence contains one of the better insults directed at Potter. After George figures out that Potter has it in for the Building & Loan, he calls Potter a "scurvy little spider." Other disparaging remarks directed at Potter include an "old money-grubbing buzzard" (George); a "warped, frustrated old man" (George); "a hard-skulled character" (Peter Bailey); and ". . . a sick man. Frustrated and sick. Sick in his mind, sick in his soul, if he has one" (Peter Bailey).

Mary's on the Nest *(1:12:42)*

RANDOM THOUGHTS: When George arrives home from his meeting with Potter, Mary is already in bed and a clock on the nightstand reads 12:25 A.M. *(1:14:26)* Hmmm. Do you think George might have stopped by Martini's for a couple of pops to take the edge off?

8

THE WAR YEARS

❝ Hold on . . . hold on . . . hold on now. Don't you
know there's a war on? **❞**

—GEORGE BAILEY

It's been pretty slow going so far getting back to present-day 1945, but
we're about to cover eleven years in less than two minutes by switching
to montage mode. First we learn about life for George and Mary in the mid-
to late 1930s. While George has had his hands full keeping the Building &
Loan afloat and fending off Potter, Mary has been busy fixing up the house
and looking after their first two children.

Next we learn about life in Bedford Falls during World War II. George
and Mary have two more babies during the war years, and we see how
George and Mary and their friends and family contribute to the war effort.
George's brother and friends all make heroic and high-profile contributions
"over there." But George is deemed unfit for military service on account of
his bad ear. He is therefore left fighting "the battle of Bedford Falls,"
assuming a number of war-related responsibilities that, although important,
nevertheless leave him unfulfilled. Poor George. Not even a war, it seems,
can spring him from Bedford Falls!

=======

The "Bailey Family" Montage *(1:14:40)*

CLOSER LOOK: Some interesting graffiti shows up during the Bailey family montage. George is shown by the staircase after returning home from another hard day's work. Behind him, on the portion of the wall that has no wallpaper, appears the word *spooks*. *(1:15:00)* On the same wall, farther to the right, the name *Potter* is scrawled above a drawing. *(1:14:59)* It seems that *spooks* was scrawled years ago by vandals while the house sat abandoned. We know this because on George and Mary's honeymoon night, the same graffiti can be seen protruding from behind the "Get a Fisk" poster, with an arrow pointing upstairs; in other words, "this way to the ghosts." *(1:01:36)* (By the way, during the bridal suite scene, *spooks* also appears on the wall behind George, screen left, as he surveys the accommodations.) *(1:01:46)* As for the *Potter* graffiti, it was either scrawled by the same vandals or by a very frustrated George Bailey!

CLOSER LOOK: Using stains on the wall as a bench mark, we can confirm a minor continuity gaffe: the section of wallpaper that Mary hangs by the stairs is not present in the very next shot when George has his first run-in with the banister knob. *(1:14:55)*

The "War Years" Montage *(1:15:08)*

DID YOU KNOW? Kicking off the war montage is a sign that reads "Checking Station—Recruit Reception Center—Casuals Report at Side Door." Upon being drafted (or volunteering), selectees were instructed to report to one of several "reception centers" scattered around the country. The next clip shows selectees marching at an actual reception center. *(1:15:11)* Based on the terrain and buildings, we suspect that this particular reception center is Camp Upton located in Long Island, New York. Camp Upton was one of the largest reception centers on the East Coast, and Harry, Marty, Bert, and Ernie, all being from New York, almost certainly would have reported there.

Here's what would have been in store for Harry, Marty, Bert, and Ernie at the reception center. Upon arriving by train, they would first have been shuttled to an aforementioned "checking station" (basically a large warehouse) for roll call, a physical examination, and assignment to a company and barrack. The selectees (or "jeeps" as they were called) shown marching in the montage have in all likelihood just left the checking station and are headed to their new barracks—notice that they are all still in civilian clothes and are still carrying their personal travel bags. *(1:15:11)*

Next, our guys would have taken an IQ test and endured the obligatory military lectures on sex and personal hygiene. Then they would have

been whisked off to a processing building for interviews designed to assess their qualifications and ensure that they received an appropriate military assignment. Finally, after being issued their uniforms, they would have had a few days of downtime awaiting orders to ship out to a training camp.

HISTORY LESSON: How exactly did Harry, Marty, Bert, and Ernie become eligible for military service in the first place, you ask? In September 1940, more than a year before America entered World War II, they all would have been subject to a federal draft law known as the Selective Training and Service Act. The act originally required all men between the ages of twenty-one and thirty-six to register. During the war, registration was gradually expanded to all men between eighteen and sixty-five. Of the more than 16 million who entered the military during World War II, 10 million did so courtesy of the act.

MUSIC NOTES: The song accompanying the beginning of the war years montage is a popular World War II number, "This Is the Army, Mr. Jones." The song was written by Irving Berlin for the 1942 musical play *This Is the Army*, which was later made into a film. The basic tongue-in-cheek message from this soldier's lament: Hey, bub, this is the army, not the Waldorf Hotel—no private rooms, no housemaids, and you sure as heck ain't getting breakfast in bed.

DID YOU KNOW? Mrs. Bailey and Mrs. Hatch contribute to the war effort by sewing for the Red Cross. As volunteers for the Red Cross, Mrs. Bailey and Mrs. Hatch had plenty of company. In 1945 over seven million Americans were registered as Red Cross volunteers. Mrs. Bailey and Mrs. Hatch most likely were members of the Production Corps of the Red Cross' Volunteer Special Services, which was responsible for, among other things, repairing millions of pieces of clothing during the war.

DID YOU KNOW? Despite having to care for her growing family, Mary found time to run Bedford Falls' USO chapter. The United Services Organization was formed back in 1941 by six or so organizations (including the Salvation Army, the YMCA, and the YWCA), with the goal of providing social services to military personnel and their families. In the montage she is shown serving doughnuts and refreshments to travel-weary servicemen at the train station, a typical service provided by the USO.

FILM ANECDOTES: Conspicuously absent from the montage is Violet Bick. In fact, the script as it stood prior to filming did account for Violet's goings-on during the war years. Violet was to be shown in a park surrounded by sailors with the voice-over explaining that she "joined the Waves [a Navy women's volunteer corps—short for Women Accepted for Volunteer Emergency Services] until they found her kind of morale building would sink the navy." Though it appears that this montage piece was actually shot, the "bad taste" factor was enough to prevent it from making it into the film.

HISTORY LESSON: During Sam Wainwright's segment of the war years montage, check out the female factory workers carrying airplane hoods on their heads—the one girl is cracking up pretty good. *(1:15:25)* In stark contrast to the Great Depression era, where women were urged to give up their jobs to men, the onset of World War II pressed millions of women into the workforce to fill vacancies left by male draftees.

From 1940 to 1945, the percentage of females in the national work-force rose from 25 percent to 36 percent, with many women performing jobs that had traditionally been held only by men. Indeed, the need for women factory workers led to the creation of an iconic female figure dubbed "Rosie the Riveter." The workforce contribution of American women was crucial to the war cause as it enabled America to maintain wartime productivity. But at war's end, existing social mores led most women to relinquish their jobs to returning servicemen.

DID YOU KNOW? Potter is shown reviewing draft registration papers and assigning draft classifications. For each one he declares, "1A," which means that the person is fit for general military service. Later on in the montage we learn that George received a draft classification of 4F on account of his bad ear. 4F means the person is physically, mentally, or morally unfit for service. While George probably was hoping to receive a 1A classification (if for no other reason than to finally escape from the town he loves to hate), this is the one time where Potter actually does him a favor by correctly designating him as 4F, thus keeping him out of harm's way.

In case you're wondering, other potential draft classifications included 1B—fit for limited military service; 1C—members of the armed forces; 1D—students fit for general military service; 1E—students fit for limited military service; 2A—deferred for critical civilian work; 3A—deferred for dependents; 4A—already served in the armed forces; 4B—deferred by law; 4C—alien; 4D—minister; and 4E—conscientious objector.

DID YOU KNOW? As head of the local draft board overseeing Bedford Falls, Potter wielded considerable power. The World War II draft system included the formation of over 6,000 local draft boards, which were responsible for, among other things, registering men and determining their eligibility. While decisions of local boards were subject to review by a network of appeal boards, as a practical matter the ultimate military fate of a potential draftee was decided by the likes of Potter.

CLOSER LOOK: Mr. Gower and Uncle Billy, we are told, do their part by selling war bonds. While that may well have been the case, in the accompanying footage Mr. Gower is shown stumping with Mr. Martini and another guy who to us doesn't look much like Uncle Billy. *(1:15:38)* In any event, check out the platform that the men use—it's an army tank, parked right outside the county court house. Fear not! In case of a German invasion, Bedford Falls is prepared for battle!

HISTORY LESSON: War bonds were a critical source of government financing during World War II. With the national deficit rising sharply during the war, the government obtained half of the necessary funding for the war from war bonds. (The rest came mainly from increases in corporate and personal income taxes.) Through the War Finance Committee, which was in charge of the sale of bonds, the government raised nearly $200 billion.

Buying a war bond was a somewhat involved process. First you bought war bond stamps in various denominations (10 cents, 25 cents, 50 cents, etc.). Then you pasted the stamps into booklets until you had $18.75 worth of stamps. Then you traded in a full booklet for your war bond, which in *ten years* would be worth $25.

No American, it seems, was exempt from purchasing war bonds. Some 80 million people participated in the program. And in classrooms across the country, it was a weekly ritual for school children to purchase stamps with any small change they could get their hands on and paste them into their booklets.

DID YOU KNOW? We are told that, while serving in North Africa, Bert the cop earned the Silver Star. Awarded for gallantry in action performed with marked distinction, the Silver Star was, at the time of Bert's service, America's fourth highest military honor (after the Medal of Honor, the Distinguished Service Cross, and the Distinguished Service Medal). The fact that Bert was wounded in North Africa means that he also would have received the Purple Heart.

HISTORY LESSON: While the North Africa campaign of World War II is not as well known as the Western Europe and Pacific campaigns, it played a crucial role in shifting momentum in favor of the Allies and ultimately paved the way to Allied victory. The Allies sought control of North Africa to open up a strategically desirable "second front" in Western Europe via the Mediterranean Sea. For the Axis powers the gem was Egypt, which offered oil fields and the Suez Canal—a key strategic shortcut to the Far East.

In the summer of 1942, things were looking pretty grim for the Allies when Axis forces pounded the British in Libya and forged eastward, deep into Egypt. But the British hung tough, and by October had turned the tables, forcing the enemy into a full retreat back through Libya.

One month later, the Americans got into the mix, coordinating with the British three huge land invasions to the west of Axis forces, one in Morocco (near Casablanca) and two in Algeria (at Oran and Algiers). Converging now from the east and west, the Allies cornered Axis forces in Tunisia, and by May 1943 had ousted them from North Africa. And with that, the Allies turned their attention to opening up the aforementioned "second front," a process that kicked off in July 1943 with the invasion of Sicily.

HISTORY LESSON: The only thing we learn about Ernie's war experience is that he parachuted into France. If he did so on D-Day (June 6, 1944) he would have been a member of either the 101st or the 82nd U.S. Airborne Division. Over 13,000 paratroopers from these two divisions participated in the drop, which was complicated by low visibility, heavy German antiaircraft artillery, flooded landing zones, and gear that weighed nearly as much as the paratroopers themselves. Casualties were high—some 2,500 between the two divisions on D-Day alone—so Ernie could have used a guardian angel of his own to get through this mission unscathed.

HISTORY LESSON: As for Marty Hatch, we learn that he fought in Western Europe and helped capture "Remagen Bridge." In so doing, Marty participated in one of the more storied battles of World War II. We note first, however, another film gaffe. While the bridge was in fact located in the town of Remagen, Germany, its actual name was the Ludendorff Bridge; that's why the Allies referred to it as "the Bridge *at* Remagen."

The bridge was strategically significant as it spanned the Rhine River, which in the spring of 1945 had become a natural barrier between advancing Allied troops and the retreating German Third Reich. As the Germans moved east across the Rhine, they systematically destroyed bridges to inhibit Allied pursuit.

However, on March 7, 1945, an American armored division discovered to its amazement a railway bridge in Remagen still standing. Although the division was supposed to remain on the west side of the Rhine, the opportunity proved too great to pass up, and the division seized the bridge and secured the area immediately east of it. For ten days, the Americans held the bridge intact, enabling troops and heavy equipment to cross the Rhine. By the time the bridge collapsed, the Americans had constructed backup pontoon bridges and established significant footholds east of the Rhine.

Capturing the bridge was a huge strategic coup in that it enabled Allied forces to quickly surround and capture several hundred thousand German troops and, in consequence, shortened the war. For that reason, General Eisenhower declared the bridge to be "worth its weight in gold." By the way, photos of the bridge confirm that the footage in the film showing troops crossing the bridge is authentic (except for Marty, of course).

CLOSER LOOK: Marty apparently led a charmed life during the war. Check out the back of his helmet—it appears to have been struck by a bullet. *(1:15:49)*

RANDOM THOUGHTS: While Harry's downing of fifteen enemy planes is impressive by any standard, his numbers are well short of those posted by the real-life flying aces of World War II. The record for downed enemy planes during World War II was set by Richard Bong of Poplar, Wisconsin, who took out forty during the Pacific Campaign before being discharged in 1944. Ironically, after surviving hundreds of combat missions, Bong was killed in a routine test flight just months after returning home.

CLOSER LOOK: As Harry heads out the door on his next mission, the weather board next to him announces a temperature of 83 degrees and a dew point of 73; the forecast calls for "increasing cloudiness . . . in the area." *(1:15:55)* Let's be careful out there, Harry!

FILM ANECDOTES: You may have already guessed that the footage accompanying Harry's montage segment is real World War II footage. But what you surely didn't know is that the footage was borrowed from another film, *The Fighting Lady* (1944). The film is a navy wartime documentary about life aboard an American aircraft carrier as it battled its way through the Pacific theater from July 1943 to June 1944. Shot entirely in color, the film is chockablock with amazing footage of American bombing raids, dogfights with Japanese Zeros, and surprise Japanese air attacks. Most of the film's footage came from the USS *Yorktown*, including all four clips that appear in *It's a Wonderful Life*.

The first of the four clips shows Harry (through the wonders of a process shot) heading out onto the flight deck with his fellow *Yorktown* pilots. The next clip, filmed from the nose of a *Yorktown* plane (perhaps Harry's), shows a Japanese fighter plane being shot down during a battle known as the Great Marianas Turkey Shoot. The Americans downed well over 300 Japanese planes during the battle, so Harry surely got a few of his fifteen here.

The last two clips are from a surprise attack on the *Yorktown* by a swarm of Japanese torpedo planes, which means that Harry and his fellow pilots would have been stuck on the flight deck for this action. The first of these shows a torpedo plane being relentlessly strafed as it bores down on the *Yorktown*. (For some inexplicable reason this particular plane and a couple of others failed to drop their torpedoes, else the *Yorktown* would have been in a heap of trouble.) The next shows a *Yorktown* crewman cheering as an enemy plane heads into the drink in a ball of fire.

HISTORY LESSON: Following Harry's exploits, the montage shows George serving as a war ration administrator, distributing ration coupons for tires and gasoline to a crowd of anxious Bedford Fallsians. In this capacity, George would have worked for the Office of Price Administration, as can be seen on the window behind him. *(1:16:12)* The OPA was a federal agency established in 1941 for the purpose of preventing inflation during the war. The OPA created ceiling prices for various commodities and also had the power to ration scarce commodities such as gasoline, tires, and coffee. Gas rationing was a particular source of anxiety as those stuck with a lower tier ration book had to get by on just a few gallons of gas per week.

HISTORY LESSON: Next George is shown performing another thankless wartime job—that of the air raid warden. Concern over enemy bombing raids led to the creation of the Civil Defense Administration. This agency was responsible for coordinating and implementing townwide blackouts, which, in the days before radar, were intended to thwart the ability of enemy planes to navigate and locate their targets. Typically, every neighborhood had its own air raid warden, who was responsible for patrolling the neighborhood during blackout drills to ensure compliance.

Sporting the standard issue arm band and World War I–style "dough-boy" helmet, George is shown bringing a "light violation" to the attention of a slightly perturbed neighbor. *(1:16:18)* Any light visible from the street, even the faintest glow from a radio, would invite a knock on the door from a fastidious warden. To alleviate the inconvenience, many folks installed blackout curtains in a designated room; otherwise you were resigned to sitting in the dark until you received the "all clear" signal.

CLOSER LOOK: The montage contains stock footage of what a banner identifies as an "Official Rubber Collection Depot." This particular rubber collection depot appears to have been in Washington, D.C.—look for the Capitol in the background on the left. *(1:16:31)* Also on the banner is the slogan "Get in the Scrap." This slogan was created by the Office of Emergency Management to encourage wartime donation of metals, paper, rags, and rubber. Another popular conservation program called for Americans to plant "Victory Gardens" as a means of decreasing the demand for certain food staples. While some programs had more direct relevance to the war than others, as a whole the programs were a huge success as morale boosters, giving Americans at home a sense of contributing to the war effort.

HISTORY LESSON: Joseph explains that, like everyone else, George "wept and prayed" on "VE-Day" and "VJ-Day." *VE-Day* stands for "Victory in Europe," which took place on May 8, 1945, the day after the Germans officially surrendered. *VJ-Day* stands for "Victory over Japan," and actually can legit-imately refer to three different days: August 14, 1945, the date (U.S. time) on which President Truman announced Japan's unconditional surrender; August 15, 1945, the date in Asia and Europe at the time of President Truman's announcement; and September 2, 1945, the date Japan signed the surrender agreement. August 14 is probably the most commonly recognized of the three, but if we're being technical, September 2 gets the nod since President Truman officially declared that day to be VJ-Day in a national radio address.

HISTORY LESSON: The last piece of the montage shows a church calendar calling for "special prayers" on Sunday, August 19, 1945, "as requested by President Truman." *(1:16:39)* Sure enough, our research revealed that on August 16, 1945, Truman issued a proclamation that designated August 19 (the first Sunday after Japan's unofficial surrender) as "a day of prayer" and called upon Americans "to dedicate this day of prayer to the memory of those who have given their lives to make possible our victory."

CAST ANECDOTES: Just like George and Mary Bailey, Jimmy Stewart and Donna Reed both made substantial contributions to the war effort. Among Hollywood actors, Stewart led the charge to volunteer for military service. After World War II broke out in September 1939, Stewart actually began taking flying lessons with the aim of becoming an army pilot. By March 1941, he had joined the Army Air Corps as a private, and by 1943 he was stationed in Norfolk, England, as a combat pilot with the 445th Bombardment Group.

Stewart's military achievements as a flyboy are impressive indeed. With some twenty combat missions to his credit, Stewart served as squadron commander, was twice awarded the Distinguished Flying Cross, and by war's end held the rank of colonel. And, to top it off, several years after the war, Stewart was promoted to brigadier general (that's a one-star general) in the Air Force Reserve.

Reed did her part by touring stateside military camps with other performers, providing much-welcomed entertainment for the troops. These tours would have been organized by the USO, the same organization that Mary Bailey worked for during the war. Reed also spent considerable time selling war bonds, where her charm and beauty made her a natural pitch person.

9

CHRISTMAS EVE 1945

❝You just can't keep those Baileys down, now can you, Mr. Potter? ❞

—UNCLE BILLY

We made it! We're finally back to Christmas Eve 1945. And the day actually starts off quite well for George. The town is bedecked with Christmas decorations and abuzz with news that its very own war hero, Harry Bailey, is coming home for a grand celebration. Harry's accomplishments have George brimming with pride, and George brags about him to anyone who will listen.

So Harry's coming home and it's Christmas Eve—what could possibly throw such a joyous day into turmoil? Enter Uncle Billy. All he has to do is walk over to the Bedford Falls Trust and Savings Bank, fill out a deposit slip and head for the teller's window and all will be right in the world. But Uncle Billy can't help himself—he has to stick it to that "old buzzard" Potter in the bank lobby. While doing so, Uncle Billy accidentally slips the deposit money into Potter's newspaper and hands the entire bundle back to Potter.

Moments later Potter discovers Uncle Billy's blunder and instantly realizes that losing this money would spell doom for the Building & Loan. Having been handed a golden opportunity to finally put the Building & Loan out of business, Potter has nary a thought of returning the money.

Back at the Building & Loan the bank examiner is anxious to review the company's books, while a case of the "holiday blues" has Violet seeking a loan from George so she can skip town and get a fresh start. When the scatterbrained Uncle Billy returns from his bank errand, it's apparent that he's in more of a fog than usual. Before long Uncle Billy is forced to come clean—he has lost the deposit money. It takes George about a half a second to figure out that if they don't find the money today, they will be in a serious pickle with the authorities. With that, he and Uncle Billy set out to retrace Uncle Billy's every last step.

═══════════════════════════════

George Spreads News of Harry's Return *(1:16:46)*

EXPLANATION REQUIRED: The film never definitively indicates what year "present day" is set in. We assumed that it was Christmas Eve 1945, largely because it jibes with Harry returning from the war, which ended in September 1945. However, for some reason the film's shooting schedule repeatedly refers to the Christmas Eve scenes as being set in December 1946. While the local newspaper should have cleared things up, no date appears on the front page. *(1:16:55)* Fortunately, the film playing at the theater next to Gower Drugs, *The Bells of St. Mary's*, provides an answer; it was released in 1945.

RANDOM THOUGHTS: By the way, *The Bells of St. Mary's* is itself a film worth checking out. The film features Bing Crosby as a good-natured priest charged with turning around a run-down parochial school. It's the sequel to *Going My Way* (Best Picture in 1944) and stacked up quite well with the original, earning nominations for Best Picture, Best Actor (Crosby), Best Director, and Best Actress (Ingrid Bergman), though it lost in all four categories.

CAST ANECDOTES: If you need further incentive to check out *The Bells of St. Mary's*, how about the fact that the actor who plays Clarence, Henry Travers, is featured in it? Plus, you get to see him playing a curmudgeon, in contrast to his typical role as the affable gent. Travers's most acclaimed film was *Mrs. Miniver* (1942), a war propaganda film designed to invoke sympathy for the British war cause among isolationist-minded Americans. Interestingly, Travers played the leading role in the stage version of *You Can't Take It with You*, which *It's a Wonderful Life*'s director Frank Capra later adapted for film. But Capra cast Lionel Barrymore for the part played by Travers. Perhaps this earlier casting oversight was weighing on Capra's mind when he decided to cast Travers in the plum role of Clarence.

CLOSER LOOK: No word on what the "Second Great Feature" is advertised on the theater's marquee, but the side of the marquee indicates that movie-goers will also be treated to a newsreel from RKO-Pathe and a cartoon short starring Donald Duck. *(1:16:52)* These listings are also legible when George runs past the movie theater at the end of the film. *(2:03:05)*

RKO-Pathe was one of five major newsreel companies in the 1930s and 1940s that supplied American movie theaters with news shorts covering topical events. These newsreels were an important means of communicating news in the pre-television era, and were especially popular during World War II as Americans clamored for updates on the war. As for Donald Duck, he had been around since June 1934. His cartoon shorts were a staple at theaters in the 1940s, particularly during the war.

RANDOM THOUGHTS: Forgive us for being picky, but we must take issue with the wording of the portion of the newspaper headline announcing Harry's latest military exploit that reads, LOCAL BOY WINS CONGRESSIONAL MEDAL OF HONOR. *(1:16:55)* First, military personnel well know that the Medal of Honor is *earned,* not "won." Second, the medal's official name is the Medal of Honor, sans "Congressional." Finally, as long as we're flyspecking, Harry is hardly a "boy" as he would be around thirty-four in this scene.

DID YOU KNOW? Make no mistake—Harry's receipt of the Medal of Honor is a huge deal. Awarded for "conspicuous gallantry and intrepidity at risk of life above and beyond the call of duty," the Medal of Honor is America's highest military decoration. It was first awarded in 1863 during the Civil War, and since then fewer than 3,500 military personnel have received the award.

Out of approximately 440 military personnel receiving Medals of Honor during World War II, only two were navy pilots like Harry Bailey—David McCampbell and Butch O'Hare. Of these two men, O'Hare's accomplishments most closely resembled Harry's saving of a transport full of soldiers. In 1942, O'Hare received the Medal of Honor for singlehandedly saving the USS *Lexington* by downing five Japanese planes in one skirmish. O'Hare returned home to receive the medal, but then headed back to the Pacific theater, where he was killed in combat in 1943. O'Hare's heroics prompted the city of Chicago to rename its airport, then known as Orchard Field, in his honor.

CLOSER LOOK: Here are the other headlines appearing on the newspaper's front page:

- PRESIDENT DECORATES HARRY BAILEY

- PRESIDENT DECORATES OUR OWN HARRY

- NATIONAL HERO!

- CITY TO CELEBRATE HERO'S HOMECOMING

- COMMANDER HARRY BAILEY, FAMOUS NAVY AIR ACE, BORN AND RAISED IN BEDFORD FALLS, WAS DECORATED YESTERDAY WITH THE NATION'S HIGHEST HONOR.

FILM ANECDOTES: A photograph on the front page portrays Harry receiving the Medal of Honor from President Harry S Truman, who more than once declared, "I would rather have that medal than be president." *(1:16:55)* RKO's legal advisors were sufficiently worried about having someone impersonating the president in the photograph that they actually recommended obtaining permission from the White House to do so.

CLOSER LOOK: Impressively, the Medal of Honor is accurately depicted in the photograph, shown attached to a ribbon and worn around Harry's neck. It's the only American military award worn around the neck.

CLOSER LOOK: Bedford Falls' newspaper is the *Bedford Falls Sentinel*. It costs five cents and boasts that it is the COUNTY'S LEADING NEWSPAPER. *(1:16:55)* The weather forecast appears in the upper right corner of the front page, and calls for SNOW TONIGHT. Sure enough, it's not snowing during the day when George and Uncle Billy search for the bank deposit, but by evening the predicted snowstorm has arrived.

FILM ANECDOTES: While the forecast on Christmas Eve in Bedford Falls called for snow, in actuality temperatures during the filming of these scenes were well into the eighties. All of the scenes for *It's a Wonderful Life* were shot in southern California between late April and late July 1946. Stewart certainly looks cold, but he had to be more than a little uncomfortable wearing a winter overcoat and scarf in the sweltering heat.

DID YOU KNOW? By the end of the war Harry had reached the rank of Commander, which meant that Harry was fully qualified to serve as the commanding officer on a warship. But Harry still had a ways to go to reach the navy's highest officer rank, a five-star Fleet Admiral. Other World War II navy officer ranks were: admiral (4 stars), vice admiral (3 stars), rear admiral, upper half (2 stars), rear admiral, lower half (1 star), captain, commander, lieutenant commander, lieutenant, lieutenant junior grade, and ensign.

CAST ANECDOTES: The actor who plays Harry Bailey, Todd Karns, appears as a navy man in another film classic, *The Caine Mutiny* (1954). In a somewhat reminiscent story line, his character, a helmsman aboard the USS *Caine*, saves the lives of every man on that ship by deciding not to follow the navigational orders of Lieutenant Commander Queeg (Humphrey Bogart) during a raging typhoon. One of Karns's first films was *The Courtship of Andy Hardy* (1942), in which an upstart Donna Reed also appears.

Uncle Billy Heads to the Bank *(1:17:16)*

EXPLANATION REQUIRED: Uncle Billy salutes the occupants of a vehicle that passes in front of him because they're driving a military jeep. Look for the military star on the jeep's hood. *(1:17:24)*

JUST WONDERING: Is it really a good idea, or even necessary, for the Building & Loan to maintain an account at Potter's bank? The Building & Loan is essentially a savings and loan, which means that it is a bank itself and should have no need for an account at another bank. Indeed, the Building & Loan should be *retaining* shareholder deposits and redistributing those funds as home loans. At the very least, how about finding another bank, perhaps in a nearby town? By depositing money at Potter's bank, the Building & Loan is allowing its direct competitor to make money off the backs of Building & Loan shareholders!

George Arrives at the Building & Loan *(1:17:29)*

CLOSER LOOK: Another tough day for the prop man makes for a few more film gaffes during the Building & Loan office scenes on Christmas Eve. First, George walks into the office with a Christmas wreath on his arm and sets it down on a chair to take a call from his brother Harry. *(1:17:38)* However, when the film cuts to George talking on the phone the wreath magically appears back on his arm. *(1:17:42)*

Next, as George walks with the bank examiner to another office, the film cuts again and George's pipe suddenly switches from his left hand to his right. *(1:18:51)* Finally, a few scenes later when George meets with Violet in his office, his pipe suddenly disappears from his mouth between shots. *(1:21:46)*

Uncle Billy at the Bank *(1:19:03)*

JUST WONDERING: Why is Potter still getting around town by horse-drawn carriage? Look for Potter's outdated ride parked on the street as Potter enters the bank. *(1:19:16)* The last time we saw this contraption was back in 1919 when young George and his pals spied Potter on their way through downtown. Is it possible that Potter is so miserly that some twenty-six years later he still hasn't bucked up for one of them newfangled automobiles?

RANDOM THOUGHTS: This scene contains one of the better curmudgeonly Potterisms. As Uncle Billy is sticking it to Potter in the bank lobby, Potter refers to his crosstown rival as "Slacker George." Here are a few other barbs from Potter: "Discontented lazy rabble" (referring to the working class of Bedford Falls); "Sentimental hogwash" (dismissing George's impassioned speech to the board); "A miserable little clerk" (referring to George); and "You're worth more dead than alive" (referring to George).

CLOSER LOOK: Some twenty-six years after we first saw Uncle Billy's finger strings fail him, he's still making use of them. The string on his index finger is probably to remind him to stop off at the bank to make the deposit. And the one on his pinkie? Ah, if only it was to remind him not to hand the deposit to Potter!

RANDOM THOUGHTS: The $8,000 lost by Uncle Billy is substantial by any measure, but considering that $8,000 back in 1945 is equivalent to $90,000 in 2006, there's no mistaking that Uncle Billy messed up big time.

CLOSER LOOK: Watch Uncle Billy thumb the bills as he prepares to fill out a deposit slip. *(1:19:08)* Slow motion shows that the wad is comprised mostly of five dollar bills, and perhaps a few tens. If we were to assume that half of the deposit consists of fives and the other half of tens, Uncle Billy should have 1,067 bills in his pile—534 fives and 533 tens. It looks to us like he barely has twenty.

CLOSER LOOK: At the counter where Uncle Billy fills out his deposit slip, the day of the week is shown as Monday. *(1:20:01)* In fact, Christmas Eve 1945 actually did fall on a Monday, so kudos to the prop department for getting this one right.

CLOSER LOOK: While we were figuring out the banking hours for the Bedford Falls Trust and Savings Bank, we noticed that, on the bank's front door, the word *Bank* is spelled B-A-N-X. *(1:20:52)*

Back at the Building & Loan *(1:21:09)*

CLOSER LOOK: Two war-related posters can be seen hanging in the Building & Loan during this scene. One is for the American Red Cross with the slogan "On the Job—Always!" *(1:17:37)* The other is a plea to continue giving to another humanitarian aid-based organization that was originally called the War Chest and was later renamed, for obvious reasons, the Victory Chest. The poster reads, "Carry on . . . for Our Fighting Forces, Our Own at Home, Our Suffering Allies. Give. Victory Chest." *(1:17:46)* Interestingly, the community chest organizations that formed the War/Victory Chest were the precursor to the United Way.

EXPLANATION REQUIRED: So what exactly is George doing for Violet in his office? Well, the script as it stood prior to filming provides the answer. The scene was to open with George typing out a generic letter of recommendation for Violet to help her in her job search in New York City. Look for the typewriter on George's desk. In a not-so-subtle hint as to why she's leaving town, Violet wryly suggests that George mention in the letter that "the good city mothers boycotted me and practically ran me out of town."

Instead George types: "The bearer, Miss Violet Bick, has been employed as a clerk by this company for the past two years. The undersigned is glad to recommend her for intelligence, ability and good character." As Violet watches over George's shoulder she points out the untruths, including her having "good character." All of this explains why the scene, as we know it, opens with George handing Violet a letter and Violet saying, "Character? If I had any character I'd . . ."

JUST WONDERING: Is George so geographically clueless after having been trapped in Bedford Falls all these years that he doesn't know where New York City is in relation to Bedford Falls? As George helps Violet get a fresh start in "New York" (meaning New York City), he hands her a few extra dollars and remarks "they charge for meals and rent *up there* just the same as they do in Bedford Falls." Unless Bedford Falls has relocated to New Jersey, New York City would be "down there" vis-à-vis Bedford Falls and just about every other town in the state.

Uncle Billy's Study *(1:23:40)*

CLOSER LOOK: Have you spotted all of Uncle Billy's pets? It's no secret that Uncle Billy is a little quirky, but his study is just a few critters short of a zoo. In addition to Uncle Billy's consolatory squirrel, look for the following other animals as George reads Uncle Billy the riot act: a dog, a monkey, an owl, a hamster or similar varmint (yes, it does move ever so slightly), and several birds.

EXPLANATION REQUIRED: During Uncle Billy's heated exchange with George, we learn that Uncle Billy is a widower. Though it's tough to hear through his hysterical sobbing, Uncle Billy cries, "I've gone over the whole house, even in rooms that have been locked ever since I lost Laura."

CAST ANECDOTES: Thomas Mitchell, who played Uncle Billy, had the Midas touch: nearly every film he appeared in was well received. In 1939 alone, Mitchell appeared in no less than five important films: *Mr. Smith Goes to Washington* (a Capra film), *The Hunchback of Notre Dame*, *Only Angels Have Wings*, *Stagecoach*, and, to top the year off, *Gone with the Wind* (as Scarlett O'Hara's father). Of these gems, *Stagecoach* actually won him the 1939 Academy Award for Best Supporting Actor. Other Mitchell film credits include Capra's *Lost Horizon* (1937) and *High Noon* (1952).

One of his stranger films was *The (Fighting) Sullivans* (1944), a true story about five brothers who enlist in the U.S. Navy and insist, with tragic consequences, on serving on the same ship. (The plight of the Sullivan brothers is said to have provided the seed for the story line in *Saving Private Ryan*.) Mitchell plays the boys' father, and when he and his wife receive the bad news, their reactions are odd indeed. Part of the strangeness of this film is explained by the fact that it is essentially a government propaganda film, cranked out shortly after the accident with an eye toward boosting enlistee numbers. As a bonus, Ward Bond (Bert the cop) is in this one as well, playing a gruff admiral who is forced to allow the boys to enlist as a team after they go over his head to obtain approval.

10

SOMETHING'S THE MATTER WITH DADDY

66 Why did we have to live here in the first place
and stay around this measly, crummy old
town? 99

—GEORGE BAILEY

George and Uncle Billy's frantic search for the bank deposit turns up nothing, and George returns home resigned to the fact that he's going to take the fall for Uncle Billy's epic blunder. Not even the vision of his lovely wife and kids preparing for a family Christmas Eve party can ease George's mind. And when a tearful George smothers his youngest son with hugs, Mary recognizes that something is amiss. Sure, George is a moody guy, but she's never seen him quite like this.

With each passing minute George gets more and more irascible. After some mean-spirited grousing in the kitchen ("Why did we have to have all these kids?!"), George heads upstairs to check on Zuzu, who caught a cold on the way home from school. Zuzu is busy caring for a flower, and when a few petals fall off, she asks daddy to fix it. George obliges by pretending to reattach the fallen petals, while secreting them into his watch pocket.

Any hope that George's visit with Zuzu might have a calming effect on him is quickly dashed upon his return downstairs. First he bawls out Zuzu's teacher on the phone, accusing her of causing Zuzu's sickness. Then he lays into each of the kids for, well, being kids. Then he goes ballistic and trashes his work area in front of the whole family. Finally, just as he seems to be gathering himself, he starts laying into the kids again! With this, Mary has seen enough. George too knows he's crossed the line, and before Mary can do the honors, he gives himself the boot and heads out into the night.

Probably the last place we'd expect to find George after leaving his home is Potter's office. But here he is, pleading with that "scurvy little spider" for a rather extraordinary favor—a loan of a mere $8,000. If only George's old pal Sam Wainwright was around, he would loan George the money in a heartbeat. Alas, he is overseas, so it's Potter or nothing. George swallows his pride and pleads for mercy. But George is in for a rude awakening. Potter has had it in for George and the Building & Loan for nearly two decades, and he's not about to let this prime chance to take them both down slip through his cold, clammy fingers. Before George can even get out the door, Potter is on the horn to the authorities alerting them that George has "stolen" Building & Loan funds.

Having received a healthy dose of reality from Potter, George now finds himself on the lam. So where does a man go in such a predicament? Why, the local watering hole of course! Sure, the sheriff will soon be on his trail, but when a man needs a drink, he needs a drink. So it's off to Martini's for a couple of stiff ones.

Martini's is a classic family style Italian restaurant. Mr. Martini greets his customers by name at the door, Nick pours a heavy drink, and the room is filled with the sounds of Italian arias. But George isn't paying much attention to the ambience—he needs help fast and seeks divine intervention between sips of bourbon.

For the time being, the only "answer" to his prayers comes in the form of a sucker punch from Zuzu's teacher's husband. Talk about bad luck! What are the odds of pulling up a bar stool right next to the man whose wife you bawled out on the phone just hours earlier? Bleeding from the mouth, George gathers himself as best he can, makes sure that he still has his life insurance policy, and, to Mr. Martini's dismay, heads back out the door. Moments later, George crashes his car into a tree and then scurries off into the night, staying just a few steps ahead of the law.

George Arrives Home on Christmas Eve (1:24:39)

FILM ANECDOTES: While the film itself does not reveal the ages of the Bailey children, the film's final script indicates that at the end of the film Pete is nine, Janie eight, Zuzu six, and Tommy three. George and Mary therefore had their first child in 1936, when George and Mary are around thirty and twenty-six, respectively. Unfortunately, Pete's age doesn't jibe with the timing of Mary's first pregnancy, which she announced to George in June 1934. If we assume that Pete was born in January 1935, that would make him ten (almost eleven) on Christmas Eve 1945.

CLOSER LOOK: George's return home on Christmas Eve gives us a good look at the downstairs layout for 320 Sycamore. Take a few minutes to tour the first floor using the floor plan we've created. Keep in mind that we have confined the floor plan to what we actually know about the first floor, so the footprint for the house would likely be larger. Also, the fact that this is a movie set accounts for some inconsistencies with the exterior of the house as well as with the second floor. Finally, remember that, on their honeymoon, George and Mary dined in what became the living room and slept in what became the dining room.

DID YOU KNOW? The set for the Bailey house is filled with details that give it a real sense of home, right down to the doilies on the chair backs. *(1:25:20)* The doilies are called *antimacassars* and are a Victorian-era throwback used for keeping men's hair oil from staining the backs of chairs and sofas. Macassar was a brand of hair oil that was popular back in the day. While we doubt George is making use of Macassar oil here, his hair is pretty wet (owing to his having left his hat at the office) so the antimacassar does come in handy here.

FILM ANECDOTES: During this scene the child actor playing Janie (Carol Coombs) is actually playing "Hark the Herald Angels Sing" on the piano.

CLOSER LOOK: Mary's artwork portraying George lassoing the moon is hanging on the wall in the living room just above the piano. *(1:26:05)* The last time we saw the piece was back in 1934 when it was hanging in George and Mary's bedroom on the night that Mary told George she was pregnant. *(1:13:28)*

CLOSER LOOK: Were you aware that the Baileys have a pet? It's a bird. Look for it in its birdcage as George and Mary walk into the kitchen while Tommy excuses himself for burping. *(1:26:45)*

RANDOM THOUGHTS: Pete asks his dad how to spell two words: *frankincense* and *hallelujah*. While these words are by no means easy for a nine-year-old, knowing them surely would have made Pete competitive in the National Spelling Bee. The winning words for the National Spelling Bee from that era were surprisingly easy: *therapy* (1940), *initials* (1941), *sacrilegious* (1942), and *semaphore* (1946). (No Bee was held from 1943–45 on account of the war.) Nowadays, your average adult would be lucky to know the *meaning* of the Bee's winning word, let alone its spelling. Try using these recent winning words in a sentence: *pococurante, autochthonous,* and *appoggiatura.*

CLOSER LOOK: How many petals from Zuzu's flower end up in George's pocket? Slow motion reveals that three petals fall onto the bedcover, all of which are scooped up by George. *(1:28:11)*

JUST WONDERING: Why is it that Zuzu and all the other kids in Bedford Falls are forced to attend school on Christmas Eve? And come to think of it, how did Zuzu's teacher know to call Mary Bailey to check on Zuzu's condition when Zuzu caught the cold walking *home* from school?

CLOSER LOOK: Just before George gets on the phone with Mr. Welch, you can hear Mr. Welch yelling something. The official script has the line as "Now, who do you think you are?" However, a careful listen reveals that Mr. Welch actually yells, "Hey, you! I'll knock your block off!" Sure enough, just a few scenes later Mr. Welch makes good on his promise and decks George.

CLOSER LOOK: What exactly does George destroy during his tirade? It's his work area, which contains various models, including a bridge, a skyscraper, and some residential homes. As he goes ballistic, look for his air-raid warden's hat hanging off to the right. *(1:30:30)*

CLOSER LOOK: Above George's work area is a portrait of President Abraham Lincoln. Below Lincoln, George has pinned up various photographs, including portraits of his wife, his mother, and Uncle Billy. This particular photograph of George's mother pops up in a few other places during the film. Look for it in this scene atop the Bailey's piano *(1:30:38)*, a few scenes earlier hanging in Uncle Billy's study *(1:24:21)*, and during the bank run on George's desk. *(0:53:29)*

JUST WONDERING: What was Mary going to say to George just before he left the house? Having seen enough of his tantrum, Mary says, "George, why must you torture the children? Why don't you . . ." Surely she wasn't going to tell George to "go jump off a bridge," was she?

EXPLANATION REQUIRED: Uncle Billy's phone number—BEdford 247—is typical for that era in that it makes use of a "telephone exchange name." Typically the exchange name would be the name of the town or the street where the telephone company was located. The first two letters of the exchange name would correspond to the first two digits of the phone number, with letters being translated to numbers based on how the numbers appear on the telephone dial. Thus, Uncle Billy's phone number is 23-247.

CAST ANECDOTES: Given the film's timeless quality, we tend to lose sight of the fact that this picture was made nearly *six decades* ago. It therefore should not be surprising that, apart from Virginia Patton, the film's child actors are the only living members of the main cast. As for the actors playing the Bailey children, Karolyn Grimes (Zuzu) appeared in more than a dozen films as a child, the most notable being *The Bishop's Wife* (1947), in which she shares some serious screen time with the dashing Cary Grant. In her adult years Grimes published a cookbook under the Zuzu moniker that contains tasty comfort food recipes all with catchy names related to the film.

Jimmy Hawkins (Tommy) also had a solid run as a child actor, appearing in several films and making regular appearances on *The Donna Reed Show*. Hawkins went on to become a successful producer and has published a couple of books on *It's a Wonderful Life*, including a classy photo album.

Larry Simms (Pete) knocked out more than two dozen films in the *Blondie* film series alone, appearing as Baby Dumpling in the first dozen or so. He also appeared in director Frank Capra's *Mr. Smith Goes to Washington* (it being the height of his *Blondie* run, the film credits even list him as Baby Dumpling), which undoubtedly gave him the inside track for the role of Pete.

320 SYCAMORE, BEDFORD FALLS, NEW YORK

1. Window where Bert and handyman hang posters on George and Mary's wedding night, and where Bert and Ernie serenade the newlyweds.

2. Where Mary stands when George arrives at the bridal suite.

3. Where George stands bewildered upon arriving at the bridal suite.

4. Location of George and Mary's bed in the bridal suite.

5. Where George hugs Tommy.

6. Location of the butterfly collection framings.

7. The Bailey family Christmas tree.

8. Location of Mary's "George Lassos the Moon" framing.

9. Where Tommy excuses himself for burping.

10. Location of the Bailey's birdcage.

11. Location of Zuzu's room (on second floor—across the hall at the top of the stairs).

12. Where George and Mary talk on the phone with Zuzu's teacher.

13. George's work area.

14. Where George hugs his wife and kids upon returning home.

15. Location of tables where George's friends and family make their donations.

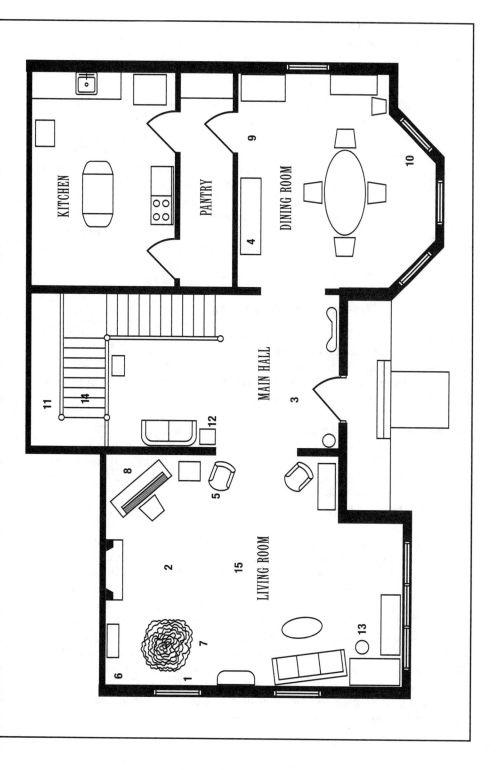

KITCHEN

PANTRY

DINING ROOM

MAIN HALL

LIVING ROOM

Nearly all of Carol Coombs's (Janie) film appearances were uncredited. But as luck would have it, for *It's a Wonderful Life*—one film where she did get proper credit—they managed to spell her name wrong ("Coomes"). *(2:10:18)*

CAST ANECDOTES: Just like the Baileys, both Donna Reed and Jimmy Stewart raised two boys and two girls. Reed's children were all from her second marriage. Her oldest two were adopted, while the two youngest were conceived. Reed and her husband actually adopted their first child during the filming of *It's a Wonderful Life*. After convincing director Frank Capra to give her a few days off, Reed traveled all the way from Los Angeles to Chicago (no small feat back then) to pick up her new baby girl.

As for Stewart, when he married in 1949, his wife Gloria had custody of her two boys from a previous marriage, and Stewart became a father to both of them. In 1951, Gloria gave birth to twin girls. Their oldest boy was killed in action during the Vietnam War.

George Pays Potter a Visit *(1:32:13)*

JUST WONDERING: Why is George under the impression that his life insurance policy is his only asset? Has George forgotten that he and Mary own a house? And, assuming they own the house outright (having presumably acquired it from the city as abandoned property), surely it has appreciated some in the thirteen years since they first moved in.

JUST WONDERING: How did word get "all over town" (according to Potter) that George loaned money to Violet? First, George had only loaned her the money a few hours earlier. Second, Potter's informant was almost certainly Mr. Carter, the bank examiner, but he could not have known what transpired between George and Violet because their conversation occurred in George's office behind closed doors.

DID YOU KNOW? While Potter may be a shrewd businessman, his knowledge of the law is somewhat lacking. As a board member of the Building & Loan, he certainly has the right to report George to the authorities. But he does not have the power, as he suggests, to personally "swear out" a warrant for George's arrest. Only a judicial officer can do that after a proper hearing.

Also, Potter rattles off three crimes that George has purportedly committed: manipulation, malfeasance, and misappropriation of funds. Of these, only misappropriation of funds, more commonly known as embezzlement, is really applicable to George. By the way, in order to tag George for the crime of embezzlement, the prosecution would have to prove that George was knowingly involved in the misdirection of funds. That means George's best defense is to blame it all on Uncle Billy.

Martini's *(1:35:25)*

JUST WONDERING: Is it just us or is it a little strange that Martini's is so crowded on Christmas Eve? Don't these people have homes?

MUSIC NOTES: While George sits at the bar, two Italian songs are played. The first is "Vieni, Vieni," a lively number that hit the top of the charts in 1937 on the vocals of Rudy Vallee. The lyrics that you hear as George prays are:

> *Vieni, vieni, vieni, vieni, bella, bella, bella, bella accanto a me*
> *Vieni, vieni, vieni, vieni, bella, bella, bella, bella accanto a me*
> *Paola, mia rondinella, sei la piu bella, sei nel mio cuore*
> *Ah, Paola, voglio cantare, una canzone, d'amore.*

All of this translates to:

> *Come beautiful one beside me*
> *Come beautiful one beside me*
> *Paola, my little swallow, you're the most beautiful, you're in my heart*
> *Ah, Paola, I want to sing a song of love.*

The second song is "Santa Lucia," an ode to the city of Naples and its Santa Lucia district. Only the first line of the song's first verse can be heard before George gets popped by Mr. Welch. It goes *Sul mare luccica l'astro d'argento*, which translates to *On the sea shines the silver star*. The unheard portion of the same verse has a local boatman ensuring calm waves and favorable winds to anyone who desires to take a spin in his quick little boat.

RANDOM THOUGHTS: At Martini's we find George in the midst of his "Bedford Falls" crime spree. With a warrant out for his arrest for embezzlement, George downs several highballs, gets into a scuffle (disorderly conduct), speeds off in his car (drunk driving; reckless driving), plows the car into a tree (destruction of property), and then runs off into the night (leaving the scene of an accident). Can't wait to see whether George can top this performance in Pottersville!

DID YOU KNOW? The featured beer at both Martini's and Nick's is Schlitz. Both establishments have a neon sign in the window that reads "Schlitz—in bottles." *(1:35:27; 1:50:29)* In 1945, Schlitz Brewing Company was one of the largest breweries in the country (along with Pabst and Anheuser-Busch). Two decades earlier, however, business wasn't so hot as breweries struggled to survive Prohibition.

Desperate for sales, Schlitz and the other big breweries turned to near beer as a means of generating revenue. But near beer never really caught on, largely because the real stuff was readily available in bootlegged form.

It also didn't help that the breweries all adopted goofy names for their near beers, like Famo (Schlitz), Bevo (Anheuser-Busch), Pablo (Pabst), Vivo (Miller), and Lux-O (Stroh), which to us sound more like the names of long-lost Marx Brothers than a cold brew.

After Prohibition was repealed in 1933, the large breweries had no trouble rebounding. In the first year back, production was around 30 million barrels; and by 1945, when thirsty servicemen were returning home in droves from the war, production had soared to 80 million barrels.

CAST ANECDOTES: The colorful Mr. Martini is played by William Edmunds, who was typically cast as a heavily accented foreign gentleman (Italian, Spanish, Hungarian, etc.). If he looks familiar to you, perhaps you remember him from his brief appearance in another American classic, *Casablanca*, where for all of eight seconds in Rick's Café the screen is his as he gives instructions to a man seeking illegal passage out of Casablanca.

You can also find Edmunds in *The Shop Around the Corner* (1940, starring Jimmy Stewart), *For Whom the Bell Tolls* (1943), *House of Frankenstein* (1944), *The Three Musketeers* (1948), and *The Caddy* (1953), a Dean Martin and Jerry Lewis screwball comedy. *The Caddy* is of added interest not only because it stars a resplendent Donna Reed as Dean Martin's love interest, but also because it features, coincidently enough, the actress who plays *Mrs*. Martini in *It's a Wonderful Life*, Argentina Brunetti.

CLOSER LOOK: Another minor film gaffe of the scene inconsistencies variety occurs during this brief scene. When George crashes his car after leaving Martini's, the car hits the tree head-on, coming to rest just short of it. *(1:37:36)* However, in the next shot the car is situated off to the side of the tree and past it.

11

GEORGE "SAVES" CLARENCE

❝I don't know whether I like it very much being seen around with an angel without any wings. **❞**
—GEORGE BAILEY

Finally, our retrospective of George's life has come to an end. The angels told us at the very beginning of the film that George would arrive on the bridge contemplating suicide at precisely 10:45 P.M. What they didn't tell us is that it would take us filmgoers an hour and forty minutes to get there! Anyway, as George peers over the railing to the icy waters below, there's not much doubt that he's serious about this suicide thing.

Don't do it, George! You can't do it! Sure, losing the deposit money was a tough break, but things aren't really that bad! You've got great kids. Your wife is a babe. What are we missing here? And how can you possibly be buying into Potter's "you're worth more dead than alive" malarkey? Are you really going to let Potter have the satisfaction of sending you *and* your dad to your graves?

It's going to take a miracle to save George now. And lo and behold, here comes our man Clarence. Up until now we've only *heard* Clarence, but here we get our first glimpse of George's guardian angel as he lurks in the shadows atop the bridge, waiting for just the right moment to leap into action. Clarence surmises that if he jumps into the water first, George's benevolent nature will lead him to rescue Clarence. Sure enough, just seconds after Clarence hits the water, George dives in after him and pulls him to safety.

After the "rescue," George and Clarence dry off in the tollhouse. When Clarence tries to explain that he is George's guardian angel, George is understandably a bit skeptical. Clarence quickly realizes that it's going to take some doing to convince George that he really is worth more alive than dead. So when George laments that he wishes he'd never been born, Clarence gets an idea. How about showing George what life would be like if he truly had never been born? And so it shall be.

=====

George on the Bridge (1:38:07)

RANDOM THOUGHTS: Forgive us for saying so, but George needs a crash course in how to commit suicide. If the goal is to collect on your life insurance policy, you want to make your death look like . . . well . . . an accident! Insurance policies don't provide coverage where the insured intentionally takes his or her life.

It's also not a particularly good idea to off yourself with your insurance policy in your pocket, as George is about to do. For one thing, if the policy is on your body when it's found, that's a pretty good indication that your death was no accident. For another, if the policy happens to fall out of your pocket, you have just complicated matters for your family members, who may not even know the policy exists, let alone the name of the insurance company that issued it. Plus, an unscrupulous insurance company might deny coverage unless and until a copy of the policy can be produced.

CLOSER LOOK: Take a moment using slow motion to examine George's improbable dive off the bridge. *(1:39:13)* From a considerable height, and with his feet supposedly on the ground, George somehow vaults over the railing for a perfect headfirst dive. We're guessing that the stuntman performing the dive made use of a trampoline.

RANDOM THOUGHTS: In case you're wondering just how prodigious the dive is, we've done the calculations for you. We timed the dive at about 1.5 seconds, which means that George takes off from about 11.25 meters (37 feet) above the water. By comparison, the Olympic platform diving distance is 10 meters (32.75 feet).

DID YOU KNOW? More than twenty-five years after rescuing Harry, George's water rescue techniques remain unorthodox, yet effective. Again, George should have tried to avoid jumping into icy waters and looked instead for a life preserver on the bridge. Even so, his dive was anything but safe. The proper method for diving into water from any substantial height is feet first—not head first—with your body vertical, toes pointed, and hands protecting your unmentionables. And regardless of whether he dove head-first or feetfirst, George could easily have hit one of the many ice floes lurking in the water, and that, friends, would not have been pretty.

JUST WONDERING: What do you suppose is the name of the river on which Bedford Falls is located? We're going to take a wild guess and say that it's the Bedford River.

CLOSER LOOK: Look for the sign on the bridge behind the tollhouse keeper as he walks outside to investigate, which reads "Avoid Delay—Have Exact Fare Ready." *(1:39:28)* The following other signs are visible as George reaches the bridge at the beginning of the scene: "Trucks Over 15 Tons Excluded," "Tractors with Lugs Prohibited," and "Pedestrians Only." *(1:38:25)* In case you're wondering, *lugs* are basically cleats on tractor tires designed to provide traction. They're great in soil, but tend to wreak havoc on pavement, hence the sign.

RANDOM THOUGHTS: That is one powerful flashlight the tollhouse keeper has there. From the bridge, the flashlight casts a beam down on George and Clarence rivaling that of an air-raid searchlight. *(1:39:31)*

FILM ANECDOTES: The special effects for the film were a huge undertaking, particularly when it came to the snow scenes. For winter scenes they used traditional methods to simulate ground snow, including hundreds of tons of plaster, gypsum, and shaved ice. But director Frank Capra was looking for a new way to simulate falling snow; the most common method until then had been bleached corn flakes. So Capra's special effects gurus drummed up a concoction of fire retardant foam and soap, which, when shot through a hose, resulted in a pretty decent simulation. The stuff was a bit messy for the actors though, as you can see in this scene. When George and Clarence are floundering in the water, both men have "snowflakes" caked on their faces. *(1:39:36)*

George and Clarence Recover in the Tollhouse *(1:39:40)*

DID YOU KNOW? In the tollhouse, Clarence does his best to salvage his copy of *The Adventures of Tom Sawyer* by Mark Twain. Born in 1835, Twain published this American classic in 1876, based on his own life experiences growing up in the small lazy river town of Hannibal, Missouri. Don't bother searching for some hidden or symbolic meaning involving the use of the book—Capra used it simply because he liked it.

RANDOM THOUGHTS: As Clarence explains that he saved George from committing suicide, the tollhouse keeper says, "It's against the law to commit suicide around here." Actually, at that time it was not a crime in New York to commit suicide, perhaps due in part to the futility of enforcing the law on a person who is . . . well . . . dead! And while New York did at one time have a law that made it a crime to *attempt* to commit suicide, the law had been repealed decades before the year that this scene is set in. So George can take comfort in knowing that he has one less crime to worry about!

12

POTTERSVILLE

66 Hey, look, mister. We serve hard drinks in here for men who want to get drunk fast. And we don't need any characters around to give the joint atmosphere. Is that clear? Or do I have to slip you my left for a convincer? 99

—NICK

George doesn't know it quite yet, but he is now in Bedford Falls' alter ego, a wild and woolly town called Pottersville. It seems that without George around to keep him in place, Potter was able to overrun Bedford Falls and turn it into a real sleazeball of a town.

One of George's first clues that he's not in Bedford Falls comes when he and Clarence return to where George crashed his car. The car is nowhere in sight, and the tree he hit is unscathed. Hmmm. That's weird.

Undaunted, George continues down the road with Clarence. By now George is worn out from all the fighting and rescuing and walking, and could go for a comfortable bar stool and a stiff drink. So it's back to Martini's . . . or so George thinks. This is Pottersville, and in Pottersville there is no Martini's, only the rough and tumble Nick's.

Now don't get us wrong—we love Martini's. But Nick's is one cool joint too. The place is packed with Pottersvillians (no pun intended), there's a guy playing boogie piano in the corner, and the crowd looks like they're ready to roll all night long, even if it is Christmas Eve! Sure, the Pottersville version of Nick could be a little friendlier, but we'll forgive him as long as he keeps the drinks coming.

To George the place is a little edgier than usual, but he doesn't seem too concerned as he and Clarence belly up to the bar for a few pops.

Unfortunately, Clarence's quirky ways catch Nick's attention, and before long Nick concludes that they're both trouble and gives them a choice of sorts—they can leave Nick's going "through the door or out the window."

Outside Nick's, George starts to realize that things are quite different. Where was Martini? Why was Nick so ornery? What was the deal with Mr. Gower? And how in the heck does this little fella Clarence know about Zuzu's petals? While George chalks it all up to a "funny dream," he's in for even more surprises.

Welcome, George, to downtown Pottersville! No small-town charm to be found here—just neon signs, glitz, and a shady nightclub every half a block or so. Dazed and confused, George desperately searches the town for signs of "his life," making stops at the former site of the Building & Loan, his home, his parents' home, and Bailey Park. Each stop offers a frightening glimpse of how life has evolved in his absence. Eventually George gets around to asking what's become of Mary. Clarence isn't supposed to tell, but under pressure from George he finally comes clean.

It turns out that Mary never married, and what's more she is—brace yourself—a librarian. George tracks her down as she's closing shop for the night, convinced that she of all people will recognize him. Predictably, George's overtures don't go over too well with the Pottersville Mary. And who could blame her for being positively horrified, what with a deranged-looking man chasing her down the street, grabbing her by the arms, and demanding to know "What's happened to us?" and "Where's our kids?" So when her inevitable screams for help attract a crowd—and the police—George finds himself a fugitive in Pottersville too.

George Heads Back to His Car (1:45:26)

EXPLANATION REQUIRED: The exchange between George and the home owner contains a curious line. When George's car isn't around, he asks the home owner where it is. The owner inspects the tree where George says he crashed the car. Seeing no damage, he gives George a quizzical look, takes a whiff of his breath, and replies, "You must mean two other trees." Of course, there's only one tree and George never refers to two trees. So this is just the home owner's way of saying "You're drunk, buddy, and I don't know what the heck you're talking about."

Nick's Roadhouse (1:46:37)

MUSIC NOTES: The man playing piano at Nick's (in a sweet all-plaid outfit) is actually boogie-woogie piano legend Meade "Lux" Lewis. (1:46:39) In 1938, a then little-known Lewis and two other barrelhouse piano men performed at

Carnegie Hall and unwittingly triggered a boogie-woogie craze that lasted through the war's end. If Lewis was thinking his performance in It's a Wonderful Life might similarly trigger a film career, no such luck. He did appear in the film New Orleans the next year, sharing a great scene with Louis Armstrong, but, after that, only one additional part came his way.

RANDOM THOUGHTS: While sitting at the bar, George asks Clarence how old he is, and Clarence replies, "Two hundred and ninety three . . . next May." That means that the 292-year-old Clarence was born in May 1653, just thirty-two and a half years after the *Mayflower* reached the shores of Massachusetts.

RANDOM THOUGHTS: If you're looking for a more authentic viewing of *It's a Wonderful Life*, try firing up a batch of one of Clarence's two favorite holiday beverages: mulled wine and a flaming rum punch. Tastewise, these drinks are not for everyone, and given what a hassle they are to make, it's no wonder Nick gave Clarence the hairy eyeball.

MULLED WINE: Mulled wines are from medieval times and were thought to have "medicinal" qualities (it's called a buzz!). *Mulled* just means heated and spiced, and there are any number of ways to make this stuff—here's ours:

1/2 cup brown sugar
12 whole cloves
1/2 tsp. ground cinnamon
1/4 tsp. ground nutmeg
2 cups water
peel from 1 lemon (yellow part only)
peel from 1 orange (orange part only)
1/4 cup strained lemon juice
1 bottle (750ml) of a full-bodied red wine

Place sugar, spices, water, and peels in a saucepan and bring to a boil. Reduce heat and simmer for 5–7 minutes. Strain and return to pan. Add warmed lemon juice, then the wine, and reheat the whole thing, but DON'T BOIL—it'll ruin the wine. Serve in mugs, and add more cinnamon (we recommend a cinnamon stick) if, like Clarence, you prefer it "heavy on the cinnamon and light on the cloves."

FLAMING RUM PUNCH: We hate to say it, but this drink sounds cooler than it really is, plus making it poses a few dilemmas. First, to achieve the flaming part you have to use rum that's at least 80 proof, which may have you carting Granny off on a stretcher. Second, for the most part you can only generate a flame by lighting the rum separately, before diluting it with the nonalcoholic mixers. Finally, high-proof liquors can put off a formidable flame, so igniting the rum is not for everyone and definitely calls for caution in a controlled environment. The objective here is to enjoy a holiday cocktail without setting your hair on fire.

Keeping all this in mind, here is what you'll need:

> 4 cups apple cider
> 1 cup fresh lemon juice
> 2-3 tbsp. sugar
> 6 cinnamon sticks
> 12 whole cloves
> 3 cups rum
> 2 cups water

Throw everything but the rum into a large saucepan and heat to simmer for five or so minutes. Pour the heated concoction into a punch bowl and add rum. If you're up for the flaming part, first make sure there is nothing flammable around the punch bowl—ignited rum definitely has the ability to set other things ablaze immediately upon contact. Pour a few ounces of heated rum into a long-handled ladle. Turn the house lights down and ignite the ladled rum over the punch bowl using a long-stemmed match. Enjoy the modest show before dousing the flame by immersing the ladle in the punch.

EXPLANATION REQUIRED: After George keeps calling Nick by name, Nick responds that he doesn't know George "from Adam's off ox." This is just a derivation of the more common phrase, "I don't know you from Adam," i.e., "Who the heck are you?" The term *off ox* refers to the ox on the right-hand side of a two-oxen team, farthest away from the driver (who typically stands to the left of the team).

DID YOU KNOW? As Nick waits on George and Clarence, he is about to open a bottle of liquor called King. *(1:49:32)* Though it looks like a prop, it turns out that King is an actual brand of liquor. King Blended Whiskey was a popular brand in the 1940s, bottled by Brown-Forman, the current manufacturer of Jack Daniels. King's ads through the years used the slogan "Be Right— Drink Light" and portrayed various folks having a good old time drinking King while enjoying their favorite outdoor activities. Who says whiskey and ice skating don't mix?

CLOSER LOOK: Look for the newspapers that the down-and-out Mr. Gower has stuffed underneath his shirt to help him keep warm. *(1:49:35)*

DID YOU KNOW? Outside Nick's, Clarence reminds George that he has no "4F" card. During World War II, men between the ages of eighteen and sixty-five were required by law to carry a draft card, which included their draft classification. (We noted earlier that the "4F" draft classification meant that the individual was unfit for military service, which George was on account of his bad ear.) And even though the war has been over for more than three months now, George would still be required to carry his draft card as the Selective Service Act did not expire until March 1947.

CAST ANECDOTES: The role of Nick is played by Sheldon Leonard, a New York native who was a natural at playing tough New York gangster types. After retiring from films, Leonard carved out a highly successful career as a television producer, with several hit sitcoms to his credit, including *The Andy Griffith Show, The Danny Thomas Show,* and *The Dick Van Dyke Show.*

Downtown Pottersville *(1:52:40)*

CLOSER LOOK: Finally, we get a glimpse of the late-night scene in downtown Pottersville. Who would have thought that life could be so different without George, but here's proof. Check out the map of Pottersville and the accompanying index for store locations as well as the location of various events that occur during George's brief but memorable jaunt through downtown.

CLOSER LOOK: Judging from the signage, downtown Pottersville is one oppressive place! Look for these cautionary signs that appear in the background as George staggers through town: No Parking; Keep Moving; No Left Turn; No Dogs Allowed; No Loitering; and Keep Off the Grass. What exactly *can* you do in this town without getting arrested?

RANDOM THOUGHTS: While George may be horrified by what's become of his hometown, there's no denying that the drinking establishments sound pretty cool. With catchy names like the Indian Club, the Blue Moon Bar, the Bamboo Room, and the Midnight Club, they all appear to warrant further "investigation." Mai tais at the Bamboo Room, anyone?

CLOSER LOOK: How else does downtown Pottersville differ from Bedford Falls? Well, Gower Drugs is now a pawnshop called the Imperial Loan Co. (the storefront signage reads "Pawn Broker—Loans"), the entrance to the Building & Loan now leads up to a nightclub called Dreamland, Violet's beauty shop (previously a florist shop) is now the Cut Rate Liquor Store, and instead of *The Bells of St. Mary's* the theater now hosts a raunchy burlesque act called "Georgia's Sensational Striptease Dance." For other differences, compare the map of downtown Bedford Falls with the one of Pottersville.

CLOSER LOOK: Here's some other signage from the hardscrabble streets of Pottersville—see if you can spot them:

- Whiskies—Barrel Wine
- Midnight Club—20 Beautiful Hostesses—Romantic Atmosphere
- Bowling Alley—Pool Tables—Pool–Billiards—Fights Every Wednesday Nite—Free Bowling Instruction—Pocket Billiards

DOWNTOWN POTTERSVILLE

1. George stands by "Pottersville" sign (shot looking toward the courthouse).

2. George stands outside the entrance to Dreamland and watches Violet get arrested.

3. George flags down Ernie's cab (shot looking away from the court-house).

4. Ernie spots Bert in front of the theater, signaling him to follow his cab (shot looking away from the courthouse).

5. George accosts Mary on the street.

6. George punches Bert, Bert fires shots at George (shot looking toward the courthouse).

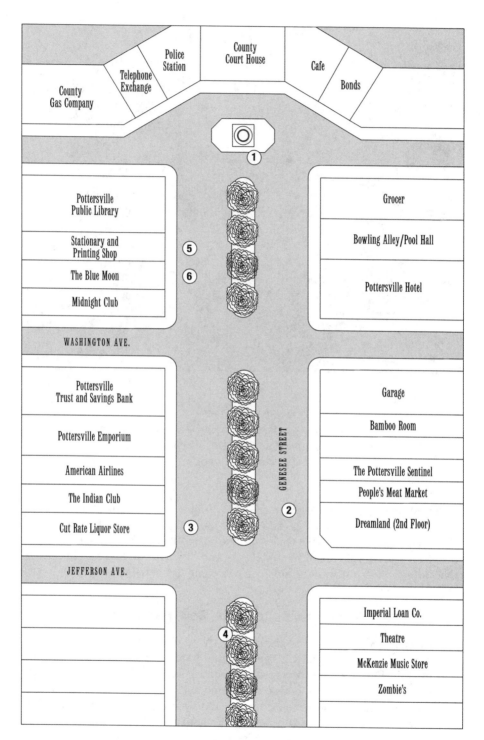

- Pottersville Hotel
- Sentinel—A Progressive Newspaper
- 20 Gorgeous Girls—Girls, Girls, Girls—8 Acts All Star Cast— A Chorus with Atomic Energy—Burlesque [note the scantily clad cardboard dancers atop the marquee]
- Zombie

EXPLANATION REQUIRED: Though we are never told why Violet gets arrested, the official script reveals that she is a "tart," i.e., a prostitute. Listen closely to Violet as she struggles with the cops. She says, "That sailor's a liar! I know every big shot in this town! I know Potter and I'll have you kicked off the . . ." One cannot help but wonder *how* she has come to know Potter.

320 Sycamore, Pottersville, New York *(1:54:50)*

CLOSER LOOK: At the very beginning of the guide we noted that Bert's Christmas Eve prayer for George is accompanied by a shot of a house, presumably Bert's and somewhere in Bedford Falls. *(0:01:41)* Well, in this scene we learn that the house is located on a familiar street. As the Pottersville Ernie and George pull up to 320 Sycamore, take a close look at the house next door. *(1:54:50)* That's Bert's house all right. In fact, the two shots are taken from the same spot, as is confirmed by the street lamp that appears in the foreground of both shots.

While it would be nice to think that Bert and his wife are the Bailey's next-door neighbors, director Frank Capra probably did not intend for this to be so. Rather, Capra probably needed a wintertime shot to go with Bert's prayer, and with limited wintertime footage at his disposal, simply used footage of another house on the Sycamore Street set.

CLOSER LOOK: While George is frantically scrambling around inside 320 Sycamore during the unborn sequence, look for the graffiti on the wall declaring "Jerry + Toni." *(1:55:33)*

Ma Bailey's Boarding House *(1:56:42)*

CLOSER LOOK: Just to make sure there wasn't a glaring oversight, we compared the Bedford Falls version of Mrs. Bailey's front porch (shown at the "welcome home" party for Harry and his new bride) with the Pottersville version. Yep, they're the same, except for the fact that Ma Bailey's Boarding House desperately needs a coat of paint.

The Town Cemetery *(1:58:17)*

CLOSER LOOK: One of our favorite film gaffes occurs in the cemetery scene. When it came time to create Harry Bailey's tombstone, the prop guys apparently forgot to do the math. Clarence informs us that Harry fell through the ice and drowned at the age of nine. If Harry was born in 1911, as his tombstone indicates, he would not turn nine until 1920. Yet the tombstone has Harry down for dying in 1919. Good effort guys, but not quite.

Also, keep an eye out for a continuity gaffe here. In the first shot of the tombstone Harry's year of death is clearly visible. But seconds later the date is covered by snow, forcing George to go digging.

Mary Closing the Library *(1:59:47)*

JUST WONDERING: What in the world is Mary Hatch doing at the library after 11:00 P.M. on Christmas Eve? Remember, according to the angels, George is on the bridge contemplating suicide at precisely 10:45 P.M.

CLOSER LOOK: As Mary leaves the library, she is holding a Christmas wreath in her right hand. *(1:59:50)* But when she turns around the wreath is no longer there. *(1:59:55)* Is this another Christmas wreath-related film gaffe? Actually, we don't think so. Instead, we're thinking that some tight editing eliminated a portion of the scene where Mary hangs the wreath on the library's front door. Look for the wreath behind Mary as she walks toward the street. *(1:59:55)*

FILM ANECDOTES: Decades after making the film, director Frank Capra confided that the one aspect of the film he wished he could change was its portrayal of the Pottersville Mary. Capra conceded that he should have made her strong and independent, and not a feeble stereotypical spinster. Hard to disagree with him on that one!

JUST WONDERING: How did Capra resist using the obvious plot twist of having Mary unhappily married to huckster Sam Wainwright (who would, of course, be broke because George wasn't around to give him the idea for making plastics from soybeans)?

CLOSER LOOK: The bar that Mary seeks refuge in is the Blue Moon Bar. To confirm this, compare the bar's facade with that of the earlier shot of the bar. *(1:52:51; 2:00:26)* Also, check out the map of Pottersville for the bar's location, just down the block from the library.

CLOSER LOOK: It's good to see that George's absence has not affected the friend-ships of Building & Loan shareholders Tom, Ed, and Charlie. These three appear together in the Blue Moon Bar, no doubt plotting the next bank run.

RANDOM THOUGHTS: George's crime spree in Pottersville is no less impressive than the one in Bedford Falls. After getting tossed out of Nick's, George stomps around 320 Sycamore in the presence of a police officer (criminal trespass), flees the scene while Bert is trying to arrest him (resisting arrest), grabs Mary outside the library (battery), punches a police officer (aggra-vated battery—a felony), and flees the scene again (resisting arrest). George better hope Clarence bails him out of this mess or he's going to be doing some serious time in the Pottersville jail.

CLOSER LOOK: After George punches Bert and takes off on foot, Bert whips out his revolver and cracks off all six shots at his disposal. Keep your eye on the neon sign way at the end of the block that reads, "POTTERSVILLE." As Bert unloads his gun, the S, V, and I in "POTTERSVILLE" go dark, giving the appearance that one of Bert's shots hits the sign. *(2:01:03)* Years later, though, Capra explained that the electrical outage was not planned, but rather just happened to coincide perfectly with what transpired on film.

RANDOM THOUGHTS: Is Bert acting within the law when he shoots at George? Nowadays, police officers generally do not have the authority to use deadly force to "apprehend" an unarmed fleeing suspect. But back then the laws were not so restrictive on this front, and New York had laws on the books that authorized the use of deadly force to apprehend a fleeing suspect known to have committed a felony, which in this case would have been battery on a police officer. Still, Bert's judgment is highly questionable given that he has no reason to believe that George is carrying a weapon, and, more important, the streets are teeming with innocent bystanders. Had Bert hit someone besides George, he would have had some serious explaining to do.

13

GEORGE WANTS TO LIVE AGAIN

66 Zuzu's petals! Zuzu's . . . they're . . . they're here, Bert! What do you know about that! Merry Christmas! **99**

—GEORGE BAILEY

With the gun-wielding Pottersville Bert hot on his trail, George makes his way back to the bridge where this whole nightmarish "never been born" thing began. Apparently one hour in Pottersville is more than enough to convince George that his life really wasn't all that bad after all.

Just one problem. Clarence, the most likely candidate to get him out of this mess, is nowhere to be found. As George urgently pleads for Clarence to intervene, Bert finally catches up with George, and seemingly the stage is set for another fight.

But hold on a minute here. Did Bert just call George by name? Is George's mouth bleeding again from that punch from Mr. Welch? And what about Zuzu's petals? They're there! Hurray! Yes, friends, Clarence comes through in the nick of time, delivering George safely back to Bedford Falls just before he is to incur the wrath of Pottersville Bert.

Now all George wants is to be reunited with his family, and he sets off on a mad dash back to 320 Sycamore, taking time out of course to say "Merry Christmas" to a few people and things along the way. So what if the sheriff is waiting for him there? George has his life back again and that's all that matters.

Thankfully, while George was stumbling around Pottersville in a daze, Mary was back in the real world trying to figure out how to keep him out of jail. Even though it's five minutes to midnight, George's house is soon packed with friends and family, all of whom are eager to contribute to George's cause. And when the sheriff rips up the warrant and makes an offering himself, we know for sure that George is off the hook.

Now all we need are a couple of cappers for the film, and George's brother Harry provides the first. Upon receiving word of George's plight, Harry flies home in a blizzard, gets picked up at the airport by Bert, and arrives just in time to give a short but poignant toast: "To my big brother George. The richest man in town!" Then, moments later, a bell rings on the Bailey's Christmas tree, letting us all know that our old friend Clarence finally did get his wings. Attaboy, Clarence!

George Returns to the Bridge *(2:01:14)*

CLOSER LOOK: We've got two film gaffes for you involving Bert and his squad car, although the first one's a bit picky. When the film cuts to Bert's squad car rounding the turn onto the bridge, notice that it's not snowing yet, meaning that Bert and the car are still back in Pottersville. *(2:01:41)* Yet the car's siren isn't blaring, as it was when the chase began.

Seconds later Bert stops his car on the bridge and immediately gets out of the *passenger* side of the car. *(2:01:57)* This would only make sense if Bert had been riding shotgun with a partner; but we know that at the beginning of the chase Bert is at the wheel, and partnerless.

George Comes Home Again *(2:03:30)*

RANDOM THOUGHTS: On his triumphant jaunt through downtown George takes a rather circuitous route. Using our handy map of Bedford Falls, let's track his progress. George starts out in front of the county courthouse by the "You Are Now in Bedford Falls" sign. He then heads down Genesee Street where in the first block he waves to some passersby in front of the library. He then runs a full block and a half, down to the Bijou Theatre. Next, he backtracks one full block to greet the Bedford Falls Emporium and the Building & Loan. Finally, he heads further back up the same block to pay Potter a visit at the Bedford Falls Trust and Savings Bank. Now the only question is, which way is 320 Sycamore from here?

CLOSER LOOK: Curious as to what the Bedford Falls Emporium is all about? It's really just your garden-variety department store, and if you hit the freeze-frame as George runs by the store in this scene, you'll learn from its signage that the Emporium offers a wide array of household products, including shoes, lingerie, gowns, uniforms, hats, silverware, and (we think) cut glass. *(2:03:08)*

FILM ANECDOTES: Interestingly, the film gives no hint that Potter will pay for his thievery. In this respect, the film breaks from Hollywood protocol, which at the time encouraged films to show criminals being caught and punished. Director Frank Capra apparently considered several alternative scenes involving Potter at the end of the film. The script as it stood before filming had Clarence appearing in Potter's office to lecture him on what an evil man he was. An earlier script had Potter standing dejectedly on George's front porch, trying in vain to join the festivities. But in the end Capra wisely left it to the audience to decide Potter's fate.

RANDOM THOUGHTS: What exactly is Potter's crime, you ask, and how did it come to be? Larceny is the best bet. While it's true that Potter did not physically take the money from Uncle Billy, the law nevertheless considers mislaid property to be constructively in the possession of its rightful owner, i.e., Uncle Billy (or more precisely, the Building & Loan). Thus, when a person finds mislaid property and retains it despite knowing full well who the rightful owner is, the crime of larceny can arise.

Potter's best defense would be that he never intended to keep the money; rather, he was going to return it once he sorted out what had happened. Yet Potter knew later that same evening (through George) that the Building & Loan had lost the precise amount that he had found. Factor in Potter's interactions with Uncle Billy at the bank, and a reasonable person in Potter's position clearly should have concluded that the money belonged to the Building & Loan.

By the way, if Potter is charged with a crime he had better hope that he's taken good care of his goon all these years, because he knows *everything*. And he may want to consider waiving his right to a jury since the Bedford Falls jury pool will likely be stacked with locals who would dearly love to pay back Potter for his slumlord ways.

JUST WONDERING: Where in the heck does Bert's accordion come from? Does he carry it around in the trunk of his squad car just in case? If he stopped by his house to get it, he sure covers a lot of ground at the end of the film. Remember, after tracking George down on the bridge, Bert also picks Harry up at the airport.

CLOSER LOOK: At least six of the Building & Loan shareholders who stuck it to George during the bank run have the decency to help George in his time of need. Shareholder Tom (he demanded from George all $242 he had on deposit) arrives just as Uncle Billy is explaining things to George. Shareholder Ed (he hit George up for $20 out of a possible $300) and another unnamed shareholder arrive just behind Tom. Mrs. Thompson (she settled for $20) greets George just before Mr. Martini makes his contribution. Shareholder Charlie (he said, "I'll take mine now") thanks George for putting a roof over his head just after Mr. Partridge hands Zuzu his pocket watch. And Mrs. Davis (she requested $17.50) appears over Charlie's right shoulder as he thanks George.

CLOSER LOOK: As Ernie reads Sam Wainwright's telegram, the man appearing just over Ernie's right shoulder is the most improbable of guests. Yes, it's Mr. Welch! *(2:06:53)* Just two hours ago this guy sucker punched our hero in Martini's, and yet here he is now in George's living room celebrating with George's friends and family. Somebody needs to give this guy the boot!

FILM ANECDOTES: Mr. Welch's surreptitious presence can be explained by the fact that the script at one time called for him to apologize to George at the party by offering up the following words of atonement: "I'm sorry, George. It was all a mistake." A mistake, Mr. Welch? We don't think so. George insulted you and your wife, and you clocked him. Plain and simple.

RANDOM THOUGHTS: It's now time for a head count to determine who is missing from the film's final scene. Here's a list of characters who are *not* there:

SAM WAINWRIGHT. He had to be out of reach, otherwise he'd have been around to loan George the money.

MARTY HATCH. Whereabouts unknown. Last seen crossing the Bridge at Remagen.

JOE "THE LUGGAGE GUY" HEPNER. Apparently it's just too painful for George to be friends with the owner of a store related to travel.

RUTH DAKIN BAILEY. She's probably back in Buffalo—a real-life Buffalo Gal— wondering if Commander Harry Bailey has any interest in returning to work at her father's glass factory.

PETER BAILEY. May he rest in peace, but surely he is present in spirit.

NICK. Somebody has to close up Martini's.

CLARENCE. But that bell on the Christmas tree didn't ring all by itself.

CLOSER LOOK: Harry shows up at George's house wearing his military uniform. The film's costume designers were actually on the ball here, as the rank insignia shown on the shoulder boards of Harry's uniform—three broad gold stripes and a star—is proper for a navy commander. *(2:08:22)*

CLOSER LOOK: On this first Christmas Eve since the end of the war, Ernie is wearing a shirt from his military days. Check out the patch on his left arm— it's a U.S. Army Air Force patch worn during World War II. *(2:07:53)* We love the patriotic gesture, but is that a military issue bow tie he's wearing with it?

RANDOM THOUGHTS: Earlier we discussed Harry's weaseling tendencies, and in this last scene we must note that Harry never actually contributes money to George's cause. Of course, he did risk his life flying all the way home in a blizzard, so we suppose that counts for something.

DID YOU KNOW? George is not only the richest man in town, he's also the *luckiest*. Despite the valiant efforts of his friends, George should still be spending the night in jail. Earlier that evening, a judicial officer issued a warrant for George's arrest. The warrant alleged that George stole money from the Building & Loan. The mere fact that his family and friends give him enough money to *replace* the allegedly stolen money obviously does not get him off the hook. Otherwise, bank robbers could sleep easy knowing that if caught they could always offer to pay the money back. So, for the time being anyway, George is the beneficiary of an error in judgment by the sheriff.

CAST ANECDOTES: Director Frank Capra had a penchant for casting actors who had previously appeared in his films, and he was true to form when it came to casting *It's a Wonderful Life*. For example, no less than eight of the actors from *It's a Wonderful Life* (actually nine if you include Jimmy the Raven) also appear in Capra's 1938 film *You Can't Take It with You*: Jimmy Stewart, Lionel Barrymore (Potter), Samuel Hinds (George's father), H. B. Warner (Mr. Gower), Ward Bond (Bert), Stanley Andrews (Mr. Welch), Charles Lane (Potter's rent collector), and Edward Keene (Building & Loan shareholder Tom).

Likewise, Capra's 1941 film *Mr. Smith Goes to Washington* also features eight *It's a Wonderful Life* actors: Jimmy Stewart, Thomas Mitchell (Uncle Billy), Beulah Bondi (Mrs. Bailey), H. B. Warner, Larry Simms (George's son Pete), Bill Elliott (the grumpy neighbor on the porch), Stanley Andrews, and Charles Lane. Watch both films and see if you can spot everyone.

CAST ANECDOTES: Jimmy Stewart first made a name for himself playing characters not dissimilar from his own persona. After several solid pictures, Stewart went on a roll, starting with Frank Capra's *You Can't Take It with You*. The film won Best Picture in 1938 and solidified his status as a rising star. Just one year later he teamed up with Capra again for *Mr. Smith Goes to Washington*, earning a nomination for Best Actor. The year after that, he won Best Actor for his performance in *The Philadelphia Story*, which many believe was a "make good" award for his not having won for *Mr. Smith*.

After a five-year hiatus from acting brought about by the war, *It's a Wonderful Life* launched his "second career." In the years that followed, Stewart proved himself proficient in every genre thrown his way, from westerns (*Destry Rides Again, Broken Arrow, Winchester '73, The Man from Laramie, The Man Who Shot Liberty Valance*) to thrillers (*Vertigo, Rear Window*) to dramas (*Anatomy of a Murder*) to comedies (*Harvey*).

In contrast, Donna Reed's film resume is far less diverse than Stewart's, in part because she was typecast early in her career as the innocent good girl. The one notable exception was *From Here to Eternity* (1953), where she was, somewhat improbably, cast as a prostitute. The film—a gritty tale of love and war in Hawaii in the days before Pearl Harbor—was a box office hit, due in no small part to stellar performances by Reed, Frank Sinatra, Montgomery Clift, and Burt Lancaster.

And as these things go, this breakout role earned Reed her first and only Academy Award (Best Supporting Actress). Yet Reed's performance did not translate into better roles, and after enduring a string of projects that were beneath her talents, in the late 1950s she made the move to television via *The Donna Reed Show*.

Several of Reed's more notable performances came in the years surrounding *It's a Wonderful Life*. In 1945, Reed had a high-profile appearance in *The Picture of Dorian Gray* (1945), which did quite well at the box office despite the fact that it is one painfully slow film. Reed then appeared in *They Were Expendable*, playing a World War II nurse who falls for John

Wayne. Her performance in this film apparently convinced Capra to cast her in *It's a Wonderful Life*.

After completing *It's a Wonderful Life* in the summer of 1946, Reed starred in *Green Dolphin Street*. The film has Reed playing a young lass who, through a bizarre set of circumstances, ends up on the other end of the purity spectrum from her character in *From Here to Eternity*. Interestingly, *Green Dolphin Street* ended up trouncing *It's a Wonderful Life* at the box office in 1947, ranking 10th on *Variety* magazine's list of top grossing films for the year, compared to 26th for *It's a Wonderful Life*.

MUSIC NOTES: Yet another falling-out between Capra and musical score director Dimitri Tiomkin concerned the film's final song. Tiomkin selected "Ode to Joy," which he viewed as a good thematic fit. But Capra saw things differently and without consulting Tiomkin substituted "Auld Lang Syne."

CLOSER LOOK: George's friends are even more generous than you think! Pause the film on Clarence's literary gift as it rests in a pile of money and you can see a couple of $100 bills and even a $1,000 bill. So who among George's friends is the true "angel" donor?

CLOSER LOOK: You be the judge as to whether Ward Bond is actually playing that accordion; we say yes. Whatever the case, if you listen closely you can definitely hear an accordion playing during "Auld Lang Syne."

CLOSER LOOK: Clarence's inscription in *The Adventures of Tom Sawyer* reads:

Dear George:

Remember no man is a failure who has friends.
Thanks for the wings!

Love
Clarence

CLOSER LOOK: Watch Zuzu as she struggles mightily with the words to "Auld Lang Syne." Apparently, someone forgot to tell poor Karolyn Grimes what the words were!

MUSIC NOTES: Who can blame little Zuzu for not knowing the words? Year after year people feel their way through this song without knowing what they're actually singing about. Well, in a nutshell, it's an old Scottish song that is meant to recall times gone by. *Auld lang syne* literally translates to "old long ago." There are several verses to the song, but here are the ones that we're accustomed to singing:

Should old acquaintance be forgot
And never brought to mind?
Should old acquaintance be forgot
And days of auld lang syne?

For auld lang syne, my dear
For auld lang syne
We'll take/drink a cup of kindness yet
For auld lang syne.

The message here? Let's all take a moment to remember the friends we've made through the years. Well, on this Christmas Eve, that is something George will gladly do!

THE MUSICAL SCORE

We've provided two song lists relating to the film's musical score. The first contains popular songs that were used in the score, along with an explanation of where the songs appear. The second contains the original cues by the film's musical score director, Dimitri Tiomkin, along with an explanation of how the cues were used (or not used, as the case often was) in the film.

Popular Song Cues

"Buffalo Gals" (unknown)—played throughout the film.

"Adeste Fidelis" (John Francis Wade)—played in the opening scene as George's friends and family are heard praying for him.

"Ave Maria" (Bach/Gounod)—played while angels Franklin and Joseph talk in heaven.

"Twinkle, Twinkle, Little Star" (unknown)—refrain played throughout the film.

"Collegiate" (Jaffe/Bonx)—the first song played by the band at the graduation dance.

"The Charleston" (Mack/Johnson)—played by the band at the graduation dance.

"My Wild Irish Rose" (Chauncey Olcott)—sung by Uncle Billy leaving Harry's "welcome home" party.

"Avalon" (Rose/Jolson)—played as George and his mother talk outside at Harry's "welcome home" party.

"Wedding March" (Felix Mendelssohn)—played during George and Mary's wedding send-off.

"Song of the Islands" (Charles E. King)—played on the phonograph on George and Mary's wedding night.

"I Love You Truly" (Carrie Jacobs-Bond)—sung by Bert and Ernie on George and Mary's wedding night.

"O Sole Mio" (Di Capua/Mazzucchi/Capurro)—played as the Martinis arrive at Bailey Park.

"This Is the Army Mr. Jones" (Irving Berlin)—played during the "war years" montage.

"Dankgebet" (unknown)—played during the "war years" montage for the church footage.

"When Johnny Comes Marching Home" (Patrick S. Gilmore, aka Louis Lambert)—played as Uncle Billy walks to the bank.

"Hark the Herald Angels Sing" (Felix Mendelssohn)—played by Janie on the piano, and sung by all in the film's last scene.

"Vieni, Vieni" (Kroger/Varna/Scotto)—the first song played at Martini's.

"Santa Lucia" (unknown)—the second song played at Martini's.

Untitled Boogie Piano (Meade "Lux" Lewis)—played at Nick's.

"North America Meets South America" (Rodgers/Hart)—played as part of a medley as George walks through downtown Pottersville.

"Hallelujah" (Alfred Newman)—played when George arrives home for the final scene.

"Auld Lang Syne" (unknown)—sung by all in the last scene.

Dimitri Tiomkin's Original Score Cues

"Main Title/Heaven/Ski Run"—first part used in the introduction; second part is used in the prayer scene and the scene in heaven; third part cut in full from the sledding scene.

"Death Telegram/Gower's Deliverance"—both parts cut in full from the poison capsules scenes.

"George and Dad"—cut in full from the Bailey family dinner table scene.

"Father's Death"—partially used in the scene where George learns that his father has had a stroke.

"Love Sequence"—cut in full from George and Mary's love scene.

"Wedding Cigars/George Lassos Stork"—first part cut in full from the end of the bank run scene; second part partially used in the scene where Mary tells George she's pregnant.

"Dilemma/Bank Crisis/Search for Money/Potter's Threat"—first two parts cut in full from the bank run scenes; third part partially used during the scene where George and Uncle Billy search for the bank deposit; fourth part cut in full from the scene where George asks Potter for a loan.

"Clarence's Arrival"—used in the scene where George arrives on the bridge contemplating suicide.

"George Is Unborn/Haunted House"—first part partially used in the scenes after Clarence grants George his wish that he'd never been born; second part used in the scene where George returns to his house in Pottersville.

"Pottersville Cemetery/Wrong Ma Bailey/Wrong Mary Hatch/The Prayer"—first part used for the cemetery scene; second part cut and replaced; third part used in the scene outside the library; fourth part used in the scene where George returns to the bridge.

"It's a Wonderful Life"—partially used during the final scenes; originally slated for George's run home through the end of the film.

The following quiz questions are a great way to test your knowledge of the film. We have provided no less than 166 questions relating to events portrayed in the film. Some should be easy; others will put your credibility as a self-proclaimed *It's a Wonderful Life* expert to the test. Quiz questions are grouped by chapter, so you can test your knowledge all at once or in bunches as you read each chapter. Good luck!

Chapter 1—The Angels Conspire to Save George

1. What is Clarence's profession?

2. What does the head angel compare Clarence's IQ to?
    a) rabbit
    b) wombat
    c) squirrel
    d) rock

3. What is Clarence unable to do without assistance from the other angels until he gets his wings?

4. Name all of the boys who are shown sledding down the hill and the order they go in.

5. What is George holding in his hand as he sleds down the hill?

6. What do the boys use for a sled?

7. In which ear does George lose hearing after diving into the icy water to save Harry?

8. Why is Mr. Gower upset at George when he arrives at the store?

9. What do young Violet and Mary order at the soda fountain in Gower Drugs?

10. What name does George call Mary when she confesses that she doesn't like coconuts?

11. Which of the following is NOT a place identified by George as having coconuts?
    a) Tahiti
    b) Bali
    c) the Fiji Islands
    d) the Coral Sea

12. What does Mr. Gower tell George he's not "paid to be"?

13. What is Mr. Gower's first name?

14. What is the name of the college that Mr. Gower's son was attending at the time of his death?

Chapter 2—George Prepares to "See the World"

15. Name one of the three places that George mentions when he tells the luggage shop owner he wants a big suitcase with room for labels.

16. Who bought the suitcase for George?

17. What is the first name of the salesman who helps George at the luggage shop?

18. What is the contraption in Mr. Gower's drugstore that George uses to make wishes?

19. What does George always wish for with the contraption?

20. Who tells George not to take any "plugged nickels" on his trip?

21. According to Violet, when is the only time she wears the dress that George compliments?

22. What song are George and Harry singing upstairs before they come down for dinner on the night of the graduation dance?

23. What does Annie the maid threaten to hit Harry with?

24. What does Harry borrow from his parents, over his mother's objection, for the graduation dance?

25. What is Harry carrying in his arms and on his head as he leaves home for the graduation dance?

26. What committee does Harry chair for the graduation dance?

27. What does Mr. Bailey tell Harry he is not allowed to do on the night of the dance?

Chapter 3—The High School Graduation Dance

28. What is George carrying when he arrives at the graduation dance?

29. What sport does Sam try to convince Harry to play in college?

30. Who came up with the idea for a retractable gym floor built on top of a swimming pool?

31. Who cajoles George into dancing with Mary?

32. As George approaches Mary at the dance, Mary's dance partner is telling a story about a race that he lost. What place does he say he came in and why did he lose?

33. What song is playing for George and Mary's first dance together?

34. What is the prize for winning the Charleston contest?

35. Who is Violet's partner for the Charleston contest?

36. Who is the last person shown jumping into the pool?

37. What are George and Mary carrying in their hands as they sing "Buffalo Gals" on their walk home?

38. What number is on the football jersey worn by George after the graduation dance?

39. What is on the back of the robe worn by Mary after the graduation dance?

40. What is the name used by locals to refer to the abandoned house that George and Mary throw rocks at?

41. What two sites in Europe does George tell Mary he wants to visit?

42. What three things does Mary threaten to do if George does not give her robe back?

43. What type of shrubbery does Mary hide in after losing her robe?

44. Name the two people who inform George that his father has had a stroke.

Chapter 4—George's Plan to "See the World" Gets Derailed

45. What activity does Potter claim one should partake in with Building
    & Loan employees to increase one's chances of obtaining a home loan?
    a) throwing dice
    b) playing cards
    c) drinking beer
    d) shooting pool

46. Whose loan application does Potter say was turned down by his bank
    but accepted by the Building & Loan?

47. How long has the Building & Loan been in business at the time of
    Peter Bailey's death?

48. Name one of the two places mentioned by George at the train station
    that he thinks would be a great place to work.

49. What is Harry's new bride's full maiden name?

50. What snack does Harry's wife offer George at the train station?

51. What type of business does Harry's father-in-law own?

52. In what city is Harry's father-in-law's business located?

53. What type of work will Harry be doing when he starts working for his
    father-in-law?

54. At Harry's "welcome home" party, who takes the photograph of the
    partygoers on the front porch of the Bailey home?

55. What song does Uncle Billy sing as he stumbles home drunk from
    Harry's "welcome home" party?

56. When George runs into Violet in downtown Bedford Falls, where does
    George say he's going?

57. In addition to Mt. Bedford, to what other geographical site does
    George want to take Violet on the night of Harry's "welcome home"
    party?

58. How far does Violet say it is from downtown up to Mt. Bedford?

Chapter 5—George Calls on Mary

59. What two objects does George whack with a stick in front of Mary's
    house?

60. Where does Mary say she has taken vacations while in college?

61. What does George forget at Mary's house?

62. Identify the characters who utter the following nicknames for George:
    a) Georgie Porgie
    b) Moss Back George
    c) George Geographic Explorer Bailey
    d) George Baileyoffski
    e) Slacker George

63. What is the name of the hotel visible from Sam's office window in New York City as he talks on the phone with George and Mary?

64. The factory that Sam originally wants to use for his plastics business is located in what city?

65. Where does Sam Wainwright get the business idea that will soon make him rich?

Chapter 6—George and Mary's Wedding Day

66. What is the site of George and Mary's wedding reception and send-off?

67. Who catches Mary's bouquet?

68. What is the wedding gift given to George and Mary in the cab ride to the train station and who is the gift from?

69. Where are George and Mary planning to go on their honeymoon?

70. What does Mary liken herself to when George hands her the honeymoon kitty in the back of Ernie's cab?

71. Which guest misses George and Mary's wedding on account of the bank run?

72. Which American president's portrait is hanging in George's office during the bank run scene?

73. Whose picture does George seek inspiration from on the day of the bank run?

74. How much is Potter paying on the dollar for Building & Loan shares during the bank run?

75. Which of the following businesses is NOT identified by George as being controlled by Potter?
    a) the bank
    b) the town newspaper
    c) the bus lines
    d) the department stores

76. How much of the honeymoon kitty does George spend paying off shareholders?

77. What song do George, Tilly, and Eustace sing to celebrate the Building & Loan surviving the bank run?

78. Mary refers to their new home as what famous hotel?

79. What is the address of George and Mary's new home?

80. What are Mary's first words for George upon his arrival at the bridal suite?

81. What device is powering the spit that is being used to cook their wedding-night dinner?

Chapter 7—Moving Day for the Martinis

82. What is Mr. Martini's first name?

83. What does Mr. Martini say his family will no longer have to live like when they move out of Potter's Field?
    a) peasants
    b) rats
    c) pigs
    d) dogs

84. What three gifts do George and Mary give to the Martinis for their new home?

85. Where are Sam Wainwright and his wife headed when they stop in Bedford Falls, and what is the purpose of their visit?

86. Who is waiting to see Potter as he meets with his rent collector?

87. How does Potter attempt to obtain a psychological edge on visitors to his office?

88. What does Potter offer George as a goodwill gesture?

89. What is Potter's middle initial?

90. What is Potter's position at the bank?

91. What activity did Potter's rent collector partake in years ago on the land where Bailey Park is now located?

92. What event causes George to suddenly realize that there is deceit behind Potter's lucrative job offer?

93. What does Mary say marrying George kept her from being?

Chapters 8 and 9—The War Years/Christmas Eve 1945

94. What specific application of plastics does Sam Wainwright seize on to make his fortune?

95. Identify the characters who undertake the following stateside jobs during the war:
    a) war bond sellers (2)
    b) war ration administrator
    c) Red Cross volunteers (2)
    d) head of local draft board
    e) U.S.O. volunteer

96. Identify the characters associated with the following events from the war:
    a) awarded the Silver Star
    b) parachuted into France
    c) captured the Bridge at Remagen
    d) wounded in North Africa
    e) flew for the navy

97. How many enemy planes did Harry shoot down during World War II?

98. When is the town celebration for Harry's return from the war scheduled to take place?

99. Who decorates Harry with the Medal of Honor?

100. What is Harry's navy rank at the end of the movie?

101. Who does Mrs. Bailey lunch with while attending Harry's Medal of Honor ceremony?

102. Identify the following characters who are referenced in the film, but never make an appearance:
    a) Martha
    b) Ingie
    c) Mrs. Blaine
    d) Robert

103. What is the name of Bedford Falls' newspaper?

104. What city is Violet leaving town for?

105. What does Uncle Billy caution some townsfolk not to do as they hang a banner in preparation for the town celebration planned for Harry?

106. What is the name of Uncle Billy's deceased wife?

107. How does George characterize the financial condition of the Building & Loan to the bank examiner on Christmas Eve?

108. In what New York city will the bank examiner be spending Christmas?

109. What is the bank examiner's last name?

110. Which one of Uncle Billy's pets consoles him after he realizes that he has lost the deposit money?

Chapter 10—Something's the Matter with Daddy

111. What are the names of George and Mary's four children, listed from oldest to youngest?

112. What three things does George leave at the office on Christmas Eve?

113. What toy is Tommy playing with while George and Mary talk on the phone with Zuzu's teacher?

114. Who puts the star atop the Bailey family Christmas tree?

115. What two words does George's oldest son ask him to spell, and how are they spelled?

116. What project is George's oldest son working on that leads him to ask his father for help with his spelling?

117. Who is depicted on the masks that George's two sons are wearing on Christmas Eve?

118. What is the name of the family that lives next door to the Baileys?

119. What does Tommy excuse himself for doing on Christmas Eve?

120. What is Zuzu's temperature on Christmas Eve?

121. How did Zuzu catch a cold?

122. What does George knock over during his Christmas Eve outburst?

123. Which American president's portrait is displayed in George and Mary's house?

124. Whom does Mary call for help just after George storms out of the house, and what is this person's phone number?

125. What does George offer Potter as collateral for a personal loan to cover the money lost by Uncle Billy?

126. What does Mr. Welch insist on doing before leaving Martini's?

127. Who planted the tree that George runs into with his car?

Chapters 11 and 12—George "Saves" Clarence/Pottersville

128. What activity does the tollhouse keeper refrain from doing every time Clarence says or does something unusual?

129. What book does Clarence carry with him?

130. What is Clarence's full name and rank?

131. Name four things that George notices are different at the tollhouse after Clarence grants him his wish that he had never been born.

132. What name does George mistakenly call Clarence after they leave the spot where George thinks he crashed his car?

133. What does George order at Nick's?

134. What is Clarence's original drink order at Nick's?

135. Why does Clarence change his drink order?

136. What special instructions does Clarence give Nick for making mulled wine?

137. What does Clarence say to cause Nick to kick George and him out of the bar?

138. How old is Clarence?

139. What does Nick accuse George of being, after he learns that George knows Mr. Gower?

140. How many years did the Pottersville Mr. Gower spend in prison for poisoning a child?

141. Which of the following is NOT the name of a nightclub in Pottersville?
   a) Indian Club
   b) Blue Moon Bar
   c) Rainbow Lounge
   d) Midnight Club
   e) Bamboo Room

142. What is Gower Drugs replaced with in Pottersville?

143. *The Bells of St. Mary's* is showing at the theater in Bedford Falls. What is showing at the theater in Pottersville?

144. What is the marital status of the Bedford Falls versions of Bert and Ernie?

145. What does the sign by the entrance to Ma Bailey's Boarding House state?

a) No Soliciting
b) No Vacancy
c) No Drifters
d) No Peddling

146. What is George searching for when he heads over to what he thinks is Bailey Park?

147. During the unborn sequence, how may years does Bert say it has been since someone lived in the Granville House?

148. During the unborn sequence, what is Mary holding as she locks up the library?

149. What is the name of the club where Violet gets arrested?

150. What is Violet's last name?

Chapter 13—George Wants to Live Again

151. Name in order the three things that tip off George to the fact that he is back in Bedford Falls.

152. Which person or thing does George NOT say "Merry Christmas" to as he runs through downtown Bedford Falls?
a) the movie theater
b) the emporium
c) Gower Drugs
d) Henry F. Potter

153. What is the name of the Bedford Falls movie theater?

154. How does Mrs. Bailey get home from Washington, D.C., on Christmas Eve?

155. How many times during the film does George pull the knob off the banister?

156. What does George do with the banister knob the last time he pulls it off?

157. According to Mr. Martini, where does he get the money that he donates to George's cause on Christmas Eve?
a) tips
b) the jukebox
c) the cash register
d) collecting bar tabs

158. Identify the character who contributes to George's cause under the following circumstances:

a) wires money from overseas
b) dips into personal savings
c) collects on store charge accounts
d) returns money on loan from George
e) rallies his fellow employees to chip in

159. What does Mary request from Mr. Martini at the Christmas Eve gathering?

160. Who wires Sam Wainwright to let him know that George is in trouble?

161. What does Mr. Partridge give Zuzu at the Christmas Eve gathering?

162. What character, who never makes an appearance in the film, also subscribes to the theory that every time a bell rings an angel gets his wings?

163. What musical instrument does Bert play at the Christmas Eve gathering?

164. What city does Harry fly in from on Christmas Eve?

165. What is Harry doing when he gets word of George's predicament?

166. How does Harry receive word that George is in trouble?

QUIZ ANSWERS

Chapter 1—The Angels Conspire to Save George

1. Clockmaker.

2. Rabbit.

3. He can't see earth from heaven.

4. George, then Marty Hatch, then Sam Wainwright, then Harry Bailey.

5. A megaphone.

6. Shovels.

7. His left ear.

8. He's late.

9. Violet orders shoelaces; Mary orders chocolate ice cream.

10. "Brainless," as in "Say, brainless . . ."

11. Bali.

12. A canary.

13. Emil (as shown on the telegram).

14. Hammerton College (as shown on the telegram).

Chapter 2—George Prepares to "See the World"

15. Italy, Baghdad, and Samarkand.

16. Mr. Gower.

17. Joe.

18. An old-fashioned cigar lighter.

19. A million dollars, as in "I wish I had a million dollars!"

20. Uncle Billy.

21. Violet explains that she only wears it "when I don't care how I look."

22. "Buffalo Gals."

23. A broom, as in, "If you lay a hand on me, I'll hit you with this broom!"

24. Plates (Haviland china).

25. Homemade pies.

26. The Food or "Eats" Committee.

27. Drink gin.

Chapter 3—The High School Graduation Dance

28. Two of Annie's homemade pies.

29. Football.

30. George.

31. Mary's older brother Marty.

32. Fourth; because somebody tripped him.

33. "Buffalo Gals."

34. A genuine loving cup.

35. Sam Wainwright.

36. The school's principal, Mr. Partridge.

37. Their wet clothes.

38. Three.

39. "B.F.H.S.," which naturally stands for Bedford Falls High School.

40. The Granville House.

41. The Parthenon and the Coliseum.

42. 1) Tell George's mother; 2) call the police; and 3) scream.

43. A hydrangea bush.

44. Uncle Billy and Harry.

Chapter 4—George's Plan to "See the World" Gets Derailed

45. Shooting pool.

46. Ernie Bishop's.

47. Twenty-five years.

48. Venezuela (working construction in the oil fields) and the Yukon (working as an engineer).

49. Ruth Dakin.

50. Popcorn.

51. A glass factory.

52. Buffalo.

53. "Research."

54. Cousin Eustace.

55. "My Wild Irish Rose."

56. The library.

57. "The Falls," presumably the Bedford Falls.

58. Ten miles.

Chapter 5—George Calls on Mary

59. The family mailbox and the picket fence.

60. New York City.

61. His hat.

62. a)   Violet (used when she encounters George the night of Harry's welcome home party)
    b)   Sam Wainwright (used during phone call with Mary and George)

c) Harry (used when Harry arrives home from college)

d) Sam Wainwright (used during phone call with George and Mary)

e) Potter (used while at the bank talking to Uncle Billy)

63. The Hotel Piccadilly.

64. Rochester.

65. George; he mentioned it to Sam in Martini's after reading about it someplace.

Chapter 6—George and Mary's Wedding Day

66. George's mother's house.

67. Violet.

68. A bottle of champagne from Bert.

69. One week in New York City, followed by one week in Bermuda.

70. A bootlegger's wife.

71. Uncle Billy.

72. President Herbert Hoover.

73. His father's.

74. Fifty cents on the dollar.

75. The town newspaper.

76. $1,998. At the close of the business day, there are two dollars left, "Mama Dollar and Papa Dollar."

77. "Stars and Stripes Forever."

78. The Waldorf Hotel. They probably planned on staying there while in New York City.

79. 320 Sycamore.

80. "Welcome home, Mr. Bailey."

81. A record player.

Chapter 7—Moving Day for the Martinis

82. Giuseppe.

83. Pigs.

84. Bread, salt, and wine.

85. Florida. They are in Bedford Falls to check out the factory that Sam is using for his soybean venture.

86. Congressman Blatz.

87. By having them sit in a low-riding chair.

88. Cigars.

89. F.

90. President (shown on the office door).

91. Rabbit hunting.

92. Shaking Potter's hand.

93. An old maid.

Chapters 8 and 9—The War Years/Christmas Eve 1945

94. Airplane hoods.

95. a) Mr. Gower/Uncle Billy
 b) George
 c) Mrs. Bailey/Mrs. Hatch
 d) Potter
 e) Mary

96. a) Bert
 b) Ernie
 c) Marty Hatch
 d) Bert
 e) Harry

97. Fifteen.

98. Christmas Day.

99. President Harry S Truman.

100. Commander.

101. President Truman's wife.

102. a) Martha is Tilly's friend; Tilly plans to tell her about Ma Bailey having lunch with the president's wife.
 b) Ingie is George and Mary's friend; while courting Mary at her house, George wonders why Mary didn't go "back to New York like Sam (Wainright), Ingie, and the rest of them."

    c)   Mrs. Blaine was supposed to receive the prescription that Mr. Gower accidentally filled with poison capsules.

    d)   Robert is Mr. Gower's son, who died of influenza.

103. The *Bedford Falls Sentinel.*

104. New York City.

105. To make sure they spell Harry's name correctly on the banner.

106. Laura.

107. "We're broke."

108. Elmira (a real town in south central New York).

109. Carter.

110. His pet squirrel.

Chapter 10—Something's the Matter with Daddy

111. Pete, Janie, Zuzu, and Tommy.

112. The family's "Merry Christmas" wreath, his hat, and his coat.

113. A toy vacuum.

114. Pete.

115. *Frankincense* and *hallelujah.*

116. Pete is writing a play for the family Christmas gathering scheduled for later that night.

117. Santa Claus.

118. The Browns.

119. Burping.

120. 99.6 degrees.

121. Walking home from school with her coat unbuttoned so as not to crush her flower.

122. His work tables.

123. Abraham Lincoln.

124. Uncle Billy. His phone number is "BEdford 247."

125. His life insurance policy.

126. Paying for his drink.

127. The tree owner's great grandfather.

Chapters 11 and 12—George "Saves" Clarence/Pottersville

128. Spitting.

129. *The Adventures of Tom Sawyer.*

130. Clarence Oddbody, Angel Second Class.

131. 1) George can hear out of his bad ear; 2) his lip stops bleeding; 3) their clothes are suddenly dry; and 4) it stops snowing.

132. Gabriel.

133. A double bourbon.

134. A flaming rum punch.

135. He decides that it's not cold enough to have a flaming rum punch.

136. "Heavy on the cinnamon, light on the cloves."

137. He tells George how old he is.

138. Two hundred ninety-two years old. Clarence says he will be "two hundred and ninety three . . . next May!"

139. A "jailbird."

140. Twenty years.

141. The Rainbow Lounge.

142. A pawn/loan shop.

143. Georgia's Sensational Striptease Dance.

144. Both are married. In the scene where George, Ernie, and Bert ogle Violet, Bert announces that he's going home to "see what the wife's doing." In the scene where George gets a ride from Ernie in Pottersville, George confirms that the Bedford Falls Ernie is married and has a kid.

145. No Vacancy.

146. Mr. Martini's house.

147. Twenty years.

148. A Christmas wreath.

149. Dreamland.

150. Bick.

Chapter 13—George Wants to Live Again

151. First, Bert calls George by name; second, George realizes his mouth is bleeding; third, he finds Zuzu's petals in his watch pocket.

152. Gower Drugs.

153. The Bijou Theatre.

154. The navy flies her home.

155. Three times. Once during the Bailey family montage, once heading upstairs to check on Zuzu on Christmas Eve, and once more later that night heading upstairs to hug the kids.

156. He kisses it and replaces it.

157. He "busted the jukebox."

158. a) Sam Wainwright
    b) Annie (she's been saving for a divorce that she has never had because she never married)
    c) Mr. Gower
    d) Violet
    e) Mr. Partridge

159. Wine, as in, "Mr. Martini! . . . How about some wine?!"

160. Mr. Gower.

161. A pocket watch and chain.

162. Zuzu's teacher, Mrs. Welch.

163. The accordion.

164. New York.

165. Attending a banquet.

166. Mary sent him a telegram.